TO: ______________________________

FROM: ______________________________

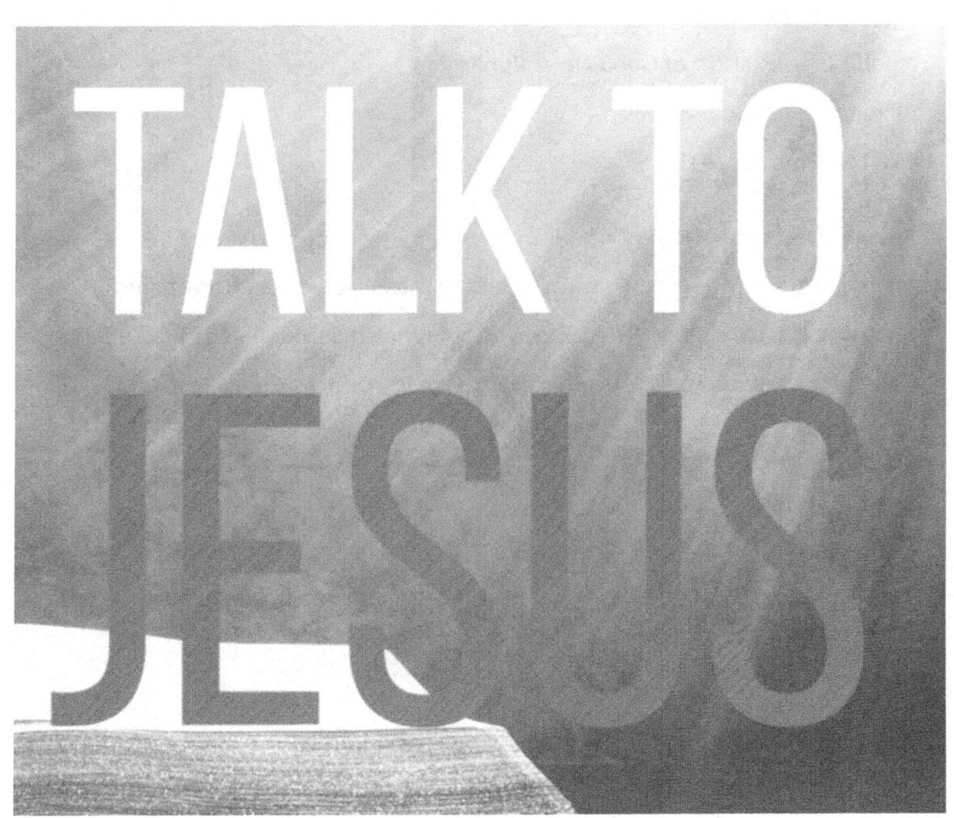

BOBBY GENE REDDING

E&M Publishing Company, Saint Louis MO
"Books that Edify and Multiply"

Cover Design by 99designs
Interior Design by Bobby Gene Redding
Interior images by Bobby Gene Redding and unsplash.com
Edited by Maggie Zehner-Jones
Printed in the United States of America

TALK TO JESUS

ISBN•13: 978-0692172292

ISBN•10: 0692172297

Copyright © 2018 E&M Publishing Company

This book is dedicated to

the millions of local church bodies

throughout the world and to every person

who desires to know and experience Jesus for who He truly is

CONTENTS

THE AIM OF THIS BOOK

INTRODUCTION | 1

TEST YOURSELF | 5

TALK TO JESUS ASSESSMENT | 8

TALK TO JESUS ASSESSMENT CORRESPONDENCE | 14

PATHWAY TO GOD

YOU | 19

GOD | 31

JESUS | 40

HOLY SPIRIT | 54

WORD OF GOD | 58

THE CHURCH | 62

RECEIVE JESUS

40 DAY JOURNEY

WHY PRAY

Day 1 PRAYER CAUSES THINGS TO HAPPEN | 71

Day 2 GOD GOVERNS THE WORLD THROUGH PRAYER | 79

Day 3 GOD USES PRAYER TO CHANGE US | 84

Day 4 GOD WANTS US TO PRAY | 90

Day 5   GOD INSTRUCTS US TO PRAY | 95

CREATING CONSISTENCY

Day 6   RELATIONSHIP | 99

Day 7   COMMITMENT | 105

Day 8   BALANCE | 112

HOW TO PRAY

Day 9   JESUS' MODEL PRAYER | 119

Day 10   PRAYER AS A DIALOGUE | 122

APPROACH

Day 11   APPROACH HUMBLY | 131

Day 12   APPROACH GRATEFULLY | 139

Day 13   APPROACH RIGHTEOUSLY | 144

Day 14   APPROACH CONFIDENTLY | 154

Day 15   APPROACH PRAYER SESSION | 162

ACKNOWLEDGE

Day 16   ACKNOWLEDGE WHO GOD IS | 167

Day 17   ACKNOWLEDGE WHERE GOD IS | 173

Day 18   ACKNOWLEDGE WHAT GOD DOES | 178

Day 19   ACKNOWLEDGE PRAYER SESSION | 183

APPRECIATE

Day 20   APPRECIATE WHAT GOD HAS DONE | 189

Day 21   APPRECIATE WHAT GOD IS DOING | 198

Day 22   APPRECIATE WHAT GOD HAS YET TO DO | 203

Day 23   APPRECIATE PRAYER SESSION | 208

ADMIT

Day 24   ADMIT YOUR SINS | 213

Day 25   ADMIT PRAYER SESSION | 220

ASK

Day 26   ASK GOD | 225

Day 27   ASK ETERNAL REGENERATIVE PRAYER SESSION | 237

Day 28   ASK KINGDOM-MINDED TEMP PRAYER SESSION | 240

ADVOCATE

Day 29   ADVOCATE FOR OTHERS | 247

Day 30   ADVOCATE PRAYER SESSION | 253

Day 31   FINAL ACKNOWLEDGMENT | 256

PRAYER AS A DISPOSITION

ABIDING IN GOD'S WORD

Day 32   MEMORIZING GOD'S WORD | 269

Day 33   MEDITATING ON GOD'S WORD | 275

Day 34   RESPONDING TO GOD'S WORD | 283

TALK TO JESUS

Day 35   APPROACH LIFE WITH JOYOUS SATISFACTION | 293

Day 36   EXALT GOD ABOVE EVERY PERSON AND THING | 296

Day 37   PRAISE GOD FOR ALL THAT HE IS TO YOU | 300

Day 38   NEVER STOP CONFESSING AND REPENTING | 304

Day 39   LIVE ACCORDING TO THE HOLY SPIRIT | 309

Day 40   LOVE GOD AND LOVE PEOPLE | 313

THE SIX A'S IN REVIEW | 319

TALK TO JESUS REASSESSMENT | 321

LEADER/MENTOR RESOURCES | 327

Individuals | Partners | Small Groups

TALK TO JESUS is an interactive experience designed to encourage unbelievers to call out to God and invite believers into a more consistent and fervent prayer life. In its entirety, TALK TO JESUS is comprised of 54 daily readings written in successive fashion to enable individual learners to use this book as a daily devotional.

TALK TO JESUS is also designed for use by partners, small groups and as a primary tool for sparking a movement of discipleship and prayer within the local church. When used in this manner, it is recommended that each learner/group member receive a copy of TALK TO JESUS and read and engage the daily readings on his or her own. Each week then, Group Leaders/Mentors should host a gathering inviting group members to share and discuss their thoughts and experiences from the previous week.

Leader and Mentor Resources are available beginning on page 327.

WORD OF GOD TRANSLATION

Prayer and the Word of God work proportionately together to enable you to experience the fullness of God and enrich you with His qualities and abilities. With this in mind, it is important to note that in its entirety, TALK TO JESUS boasts 183 passages of scripture, of which 179 derive from the English Standard Version (ESV) of the Bible *(Matthew 6:13b derives from the New King James Version [NKJV], see page 119; Philippians 3:12-14 derives from The Message [MSG], see page 291).* In choosing the English Standard Version for the majority of scripture written in TALK TO JESUS, you are presented the Word of God in its most literal form. That is, the English Standard Version is word-for-word an accurate representation of the original Greek, Hebrew and Aramaic text. Moreover, the ESV provides for you a unique balance of formal equivalence and understandability. This chosen translation of scripture enables you to experience the authority of God's Word all the while enabling you to experience the clarity and enjoyability of reading God's Word in modern language.

While multiple translations could have been chosen for the formation of this book, providing for you the consistency of a single version literal translation provides for you great opportunity to receive spiritual insight from God through His Word.

THE AIM OF THIS BOOK

INTRODUCTION

"Where are the Christly leaders who can teach the modern saints how to pray and put them at it? Do we know we are raising up a prayer-less set of saints? Where are the apostolic leaders who can put God's people to praying? Let them come to the front and do the work, and it will be the greatest work which can be done."

E.M. Bounds

Prayer is perhaps the greatest gift God has ever given you and will ever give to you. God wants to empower you to use this gift, enjoy it and master it so you can experience the fullness of God and enable yourself to live the life He intended you to live. The better you understand prayer, the more you will give yourself to it. Likewise, the more you give yourself to it, the better you will become at it. The aim of this book is to inspire you to open God's gift of prayer and experience its life-giving power and transforming ability. Through the power of prayer, everything is possible. There is no greater resource you possess that has more power to authentically change a situation or circumstance than the power you possess through prayer. Prayer allows you direct access to the One who *is* the answer for everything. You are moments away from illuminating your prayer life and experiencing the fullness of God. Prayer is the pathway to knowing God and finding His will, and this book will teach you how to pray so that every moment of your life you are in an attitude of relationship to Jesus. May God richly bless you on this journey as He empowers you with the ministry of prayer.

Below is a brief overview of what to expect as you explore the insights and passages of scripture written in this book. First and foremost, TALK TO JESUS is designed not only to be read, but **experienced,** as it invites you to become involved in what you are reading. Each day you will be challenged to take action steps toward deepening your fellowship with God, therefore this book will require more effort from you than many books you have read in the past. Furthermore, this book will become more valuable to you than many books you have read in the past simply because of your commitment to engage with it.

Be encouraged to take this book with you wherever you go— to work, to school, to church, etc. Engage with it, study it, highlight it, write in it, and pray over it! Consider TALK TO JESUS your companion for the next 40 plus days! By God's grace, this book will prove effective in teaching you how to pray, and fill you with the desire to revisit TALK TO JESUS time and time again throughout your lifetime as you seek to draw closer to God and become more like Jesus.

TALK TO JESUS is comprised of two sections: Pathway To God and the 40 Day Journey. Pathway To God is written for anyone who has yet to receive Jesus, and the 40 Day Journey is written for everyone who has received Him. Pathway To God consists of 14 days of conversation between you, the unbeliever (one who has not received Jesus), and God, and the 40 Day Journey consists of 40 days of conversation between you, the believer, and Jesus.

Both Pathway To God and the 40 Day Journey provide for you ample writing space to journal your thoughts, feelings and responses to God's Word spoken to you.

The 40 Day Journey has been separated into left and right portions—the left portion being filled with God's Word and author's insight and the right portion being filled with writing space designed for you to journal your revelations from God. The right portion is labeled: *My Personal Revelations.* A personal revelation is the arousal of your spirit that occurs as you read and reflect upon God's Word and other insights written throughout this book.

Questions to consider as you ponder writing in *My Personal Revelations* include:

> ➢ What is God revealing to me as I reflect upon what I am reading?
> ➢ What ideas and insights grab my attention and cause me to consider my motivations and life ambitions?

My Personal Revelations can be used to rewrite scriptures, consider personal commentary for the scriptures, speak to God or speak to yourself. You can write about any thoughts, feelings and experiences that come to mind as you journey through this book, just keep in mind, this section is ultimately designed for you to examine the condition of your heart as you seek to grow in likeness to Jesus.

Whether you are a new believer in Christ or have followed Jesus for many years, this book is written for you. Likewise, whether you have never spoken to Jesus or perhaps you experienced Him in the past but relate with Him no longer, this book is written for you.

Each of us is created in the image of God and deserves the opportunity to experience God for who He truly is.

This is your opportunity.

Come as you are and join me on this journey.
And whether your journey here lasts 14 days, 40 days or all 54, welcome to TALK TO JESUS.

The topics that you will explore as you engage with this book include:

Have I received Jesus for who He truly is?

Who am I in relation to who God is?

Why should I pray?

How do I create consistency in prayer?

How do I pray as Jesus prayed?

How do I pray unceasingly?

TEST YOURSELF

Have you received Jesus for who He truly is?

God is everywhere. There is not a place in heaven or on earth where God is not present. There is no limit to His ability and no constraints on His power. There is nothing God does not know, and there is *nothing* God cannot hear. With that said, God chooses only to listen and respond to every person who calls on Him according to His will and every person whom He has adopted into His family.

Prayer is a gift from God given to every person who has received Jesus *for who He truly is*. For anyone who has yet to receive Jesus for who He truly is, God says, **"your sins have hidden his face from you so that he does not hear" Isaiah 59:2b.** Jesus alone is both the gateway to God and the pathway to endless fellowship with God. Only Jesus can reveal God so that His face is no longer hidden and so His ear is attuned to your every prayer.

To call God your Father in heaven, declare His name hallowed and receive from Him heaven on earth, you must first receive His Son and be born-again. You must be born into God's family to expect the Father of the family to be hearing and answering your prayers.

As you test yourself, you must consider if you have received Jesus for who He truly is rather than having received Him for what you think He is, what you have been told He is or what you create Him to be. Only when you know Jesus as He truly is can you genuinely receive Him and experience new birth and begin fellowshipping with God.

"So," you might ask, *"what does it mean to receive Jesus for who He truly is?"* To receive Jesus is to come to Him, baring your soul, and invite everything He is into your heart so He can remove everything in you that separates you from Him. Jesus says, **"I am the way, and the truth, and the life. No one comes to the Father except through me"** John 14:6. He says, **"I am the bread of life; whoever comes to me shall not hunger, and whoever believes in me shall never thirst"** John 6:35.

Ask yourself – *"Have I received Jesus as the only way? As the author of absolute truth? As the giver of new life? Does Jesus alone quench my thirst for peace and joy so that I no longer search for these virtues anywhere outside of Him and the mercy and grace He provides?"* If you have not yet received Jesus in this manner or perhaps you are unsure, you are invited to experience Pathway To God. Pathway To God is written in the opening pages of this book so you might come to know God and receive Jesus. *Pathway To God begins on page 15.*
If you have received Jesus for who He truly is and for everyone who experiences Pathway To God and chooses to receive Jesus, the 40 Day Journey is written for you. As you explore each day of the 40 Day Journey and take action on what you experience, you will find yourself being challenged in ways you have not yet been challenged as a Christian. You will explore God for all that He is and allow Him to examine all that you are. You will develop a passionate desire to pray and begin to value prayer above every other activity in your life. *Your 40 Day Journey begins on page 67.*

TALK TO JESUS Assessment

Overview

Whether you begin experiencing TALK TO JESUS through Pathway To God or the 40 Day Journey, you are invited to first take the TALK TO JESUS Assessment. The TALK TO JESUS Assessment is comprised of 20 interrelated questions designed to measure the strength of your fellowship with God. The questions and responses listed in the assessment offer you a substantial and quantifiable means by which you can measure your closeness to God.

Each question of the assessment invites you to choose a response (numbered 1 through 5) that best describes how you relate to what is being asked. Following the assessment, be sure to calculate your final score (20 through 100), and use the TALK TO JESUS Assessment Correspondence on page 14 as a guide to help you increase your score as you seek to strengthen your fellowship with God.

In deciding how to respond, consider your heart's attitude toward each question. Responding with the attitude of your heart will provide for you a greater opportunity to experience spiritual growth throughout your TALK TO JESUS journey.

TALK TO JESUS Assessment

Circle the numbered response that you identify with most.

1. **Has prayer caused things to happen in your life that would not have happened if you had not prayed?**
   5 Absolutely
   4 I think so
   3 I am uncertain
   2 I do not think so
   1 No/I do not pray

2. **How much value and influence do you place on your prayers relative to God's unfolding plan for your life, for the lives of others and for the world in general?**
   5 I consider nothing more valuable or more influential than my prayers
   4 My prayers have some value and influence but not as much as I would like
   3 I am uncertain
   2 I do not think my prayers have much value or influence
   1 Prayer is useless

3. **Have you experienced a change in your character because of your praying?**
   5 Yes, I have experienced complete transformation through prayer
   4 I have experienced some character change through prayer, but not as much as I would like
   3 I am uncertain
   2 If I have experienced any character change, prayer has had little to do with it
   1 I have not experienced any change in my character by way of prayer

4. **Do you believe God wants you to pray?**
   5 God desires for me to be in an attitude of prayer every
      moment of every day
   4 God wants me to pray, but not necessarily all the time
   3 I am uncertain
   2 God does not care if I pray or if I do not pray
   1 God does not want me to pray

5. **Does God consider prayer a command worthy to obey?**
   5 Yes, God commands that I pray
   4 Prayer is a treasured gift from God but not a command
      from God
   3 I am uncertain
   2 God does not care if I pray or if I do not pray
   1 Prayer never reaches God

6. **By what means do you relate with God most?**
   5 Through prayer and meditation on God's Word
   4 Through prayer and my life experiences
   3 I am uncertain
   2 I do not relate with God often
   1 I do not have a relationship with God

7. **Do you designate a specific place and time to have
   uninterrupted/undistracted quality time spent alone with
   God?**
   5 Yes, I spend at least 30 minutes per day there
   4 No, but I occasionally pray when I wake up and/or before I
      go to sleep
   3 I am uncertain
   2 I pray sporadically throughout my day and/or while I am in
      my car
   1 I seldom pray/I do not pray

8. **How would you describe your prayer life?**
   5 My prayer life is exciting and spontaneous/
   I consider prayer to be my greatest adventure
   4 Prayer is something I look forward to each day
   3 I am uncertain
   2 My prayer life is not that exciting
   1 I do not pray

9. **Which statement do you identify with most?**
   5 I am dependent upon God and His provisions the way a
   toddler is dependent upon his or her caretaker
   4 I rely on God and use the talents, skills and abilities He
   provides to procure my good future
   3 I am uncertain
   2 I have worked hard for what I have achieved, and I thank
   God for it
   1 I alone am responsible for my success

10. **Which statement do you identify with most?**
    5 I experience complete satisfaction daily
    4 Sometimes I wish life offered me a bit more
    3 I am uncertain
    2 I deserve to receive just as much as I give
    1 I am not happy with my life

11. **Which statement do you identify with most?**
    5 Every decision I make is obedient to God and His Word
    4 I try my best to discern God's will prior to making a decision
    3 I am uncertain
    2 God is on my side therefore I know He will redirect my path
    if I make a poor decision
    1 I do what I want to do when I want to do it

12. **Which statement do you identify with most?**
   5   I have experienced firsthand the miraculous power of God
   4   I believe God has power to perform miracles and I have seen and/or heard of such miracles
   3   I am uncertain
   2   God may be able to perform miracles but He does so a lot less often than I would if I were God
   1   God does not perform miracles

13. **How often do you obey God's commands?**
   5   Every waking moment
   4   Most of the time
   3   I am uncertain
   2   I deeply struggle with sin
   1   I choose not to obey God

14. **Which statement do you identify with most?**
   5   I cheerfully and regularly invest a healthy portion of the money I earn into building God's kingdom and advancing the Gospel
   4   I sometimes invest a portion of the money I earn into building God's kingdom and advancing the Gospel
   3   I am uncertain
   2   I am content with who I give my money to and how much I give
   1   I do not trust the church enough to give them my money

15. **Which statement do you identify with most?**
   5   My sin keeps me from experiencing the joy of fellowshipping with God
   4   My sin puts a strain on my conscience
   3   I am uncertain
   2   My sin does not cause me to feel any negative emotions
   1   I do not sin

16. **What is your general attitude relative to what you receive in life (be it material possessions or otherwise)?**
    5 Prayer is the primary factor for me receiving or not receiving blessings from God
    4 Because God is good, I receive
    3 I am uncertain
    2 God will provide everything I need whether I ask Him or not
    1 I alone am responsible for everything I receive or do not receive

17. **Which statement do you identify with most?**
    5 People experience change daily as a result of my praying and they thank me for it
    4 People have told me that their life has been affected by my prayers
    3 I am uncertain
    2 I enjoy praying for other people
    1 I do not pray for other people

18. **How many passages of scripture have you retained (committed to present memory)?**
    5 I have retained more than 1,000 passages of scripture
    4 I have retained more than 500 passages of scripture
    3 I am uncertain
    2 I have retained more than 100 passages of scripture
    1 I have retained a handful of scriptures/ I have not committed any scriptures to memory

19. **Which statement do you identify with most?**

    5 I meditate daily on many of the more than 1,000 passages of scriptures I have committed to memory

    4 I meditate daily on many of the more than 500 passages of scripture I have committed to memory

    3 When I read the Bible, I pause to absorb certain passages of scripture into my mind before progressing further in my reading

    2 I read the Bible

    1 I do not read the Bible

20. **Combine your scores for questions 18 & 19 and divide the combined score by two:** ______ **← this is your score for question 20.** (For example, if you scored a 2 on question 18, and a 3 on question 19, your score for question 20 is 2.5). *Question 20 pertains to responding to God's Word. Responding to God's Word is more likely to occur if God's Word is committed to memory and meditated on regularly.*

***Before totaling your final score, consider giving response to the questions you marked 'I am uncertain'.**

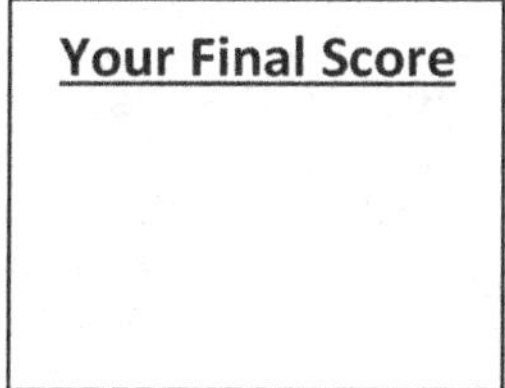

While knowing your score is helpful (as it pertains to this book), it is not as important as your desire to know and experience God. However you scored, seek to know Jesus and draw closer to Him through prayer and God's Word.

100 - 80 | Consider God's Word written for you in **Philippians 3:12-21**

79 - 60 | Consider God's Word written for you in **Psalm 27:4**

59-20 | Consider God's Word written for you in **John 3:16-21**

TALK TO JESUS Assessment Correspondence

Question # – Talk To Jesus Assessment Question Number
Subject – Talk To Jesus Assessment Question Subject
Day of Focus – Day of the 40 Day Journey to give special attention to
*If you scored a 1, 2, 3 or 4 on any particular question, highlight or circle the Subject/Day of Focus which corresponds to that question, and consider giving special attention to that day as it approaches.

Question #	Subject	Day of Focus
1	Value of prayer	Day 1
2	Value of God's Word	Day 2
3	Transformation	Day 3
4	Value of prayer	Day 4
5	Value of prayer	Day 5
6	Relationship	Day 6
7	Commitment	Day 7
8	Balance	Day 8
9	Humility	Day 11
10	Gratefulness	Day 12
11	Righteousness	Day 13
12	Confidence	Day 14
13	Acknowledge God	Days 16,17,18,19
14	Appreciate God	Days 20,21,22,23
15	Admit/Repent	Days 24,25
16	Ask God	Days 26,27,28
17	Advocate for others	Days 29,30
18	Memorize God's Word	Day 32
19	Meditate on God's Word	Day 33
20	Respond to God's Word	Day 34

The 40 Day Journey begins on page 67

PATHWAY TO GOD OVERVIEW

Which of us wants everything God offers? Which of us has the inner desire to experience God now and forever? Perhaps the answer to both questions is *everyone*. Now, will everyone choose to call on God and depend solely on Him? No. Will everyone choose to praise God for all He provides and live their lives in a way that pleases Him? No. In His Word, however, God says, **"I have put eternity into man's heart" Ecclesiastes 3:11.** Inside each of us there is a longing to be with God and to experience Him now and in heaven. Pathway To God is written for you so you might choose to respond to God's calling on your life. Pathway to God is a 14-day journey designed to empower you to call out to God and experience His response to your calling. Over the course of 14 days, Pathway To God presents you with six topics including: **You, God, Jesus, Holy Spirit, Word of God and the Church.** Each day presents a relevant scripture, God's interpreted word spoken to you and writing space provided for you to speak to God. As you enter God's presence each day, listen and speak to Him as if the only two people who matter in the moment of conversation are you and God. Speak to Him from the deepest part of your heart as you consider receiving His Word as truth.

Most importantly, know that it is your destiny to have a close relationship with God—*your Creator and your Father*—and nothing and no one should keep you from your destiny; not even yourself. Please be sure to experience Pathway to God one day at a time, paying close attention to your thoughts, feelings and experiences as God draws near to you over the next 14 days.

If you have any questions concerning sparking a relationship with Jesus, please make time to speak with a trusted follower of Jesus or a leader within your local church.

A prayer for you

God, we believe in you. We believe you are a reality worth experiencing. You are not an idea adopted by the mind; you created the mind. You are not a figment of the imagination, rather you provide the will to imagine. With confidence, we enter your presence and ask you to reveal yourself to the person reading this prayer. Soften his or her heart, and prepare his or her mind to receive the knowledge and wisdom that flows from your heart and mind. Speak to every reader using plain words, and reveal yourself to them through your Word and their thoughts, feelings and life experiences. Draw close to each person who experiences Pathway To God until you have empowered them with faith to believe. In Jesus name.

Amen.

1

YOU

You were created by God

"So God created man in His own image, in the image of God he created him; male and female he created them."

Genesis 1:27

God's interpreted word spoken to you:

(Your name) _______________________, I am the one who gave you breath so you could have life. I created you in the image of myself, *innocent and holy*. I created you with a mind so you can think and imagine, and a body so you can develop talent and skill. I have instilled in you a sense of morale so that you may know right from wrong, and so you may know what pleases me.

Take a moment to think deeply on God's words to you.

Call out to God

Take a moment to ponder the miracle of your birth. With no input from you, you were born into the world ready to experience life and ready to grow. In His Word, God says He is responsible for creating you. God claims to have created you in His own image with the ability to think, feel, create and pursue your passions. As you call out to God in writing today, speak to Him the thoughts and feelings that arise as you reflect on God telling you that you are His creation.

2

You were created for God

"For by him all things were created, in heaven and on earth, visible and invisible, whether thrones or dominions or rulers or authorities – all things were created through him and for him."

Colossians 1:16

____

___________________________, I have given you freedom to use your heart, mind and body as you please. It is my desire however, that you use the heart, mind and body I created for you in a way that honors me. Know that I designed you perfectly to fulfill the good plans I have for you. Stay connected to me always and I will cherish you and provide for you so that you are completely satisfied in me.

____

Take a moment to think deeply on God's words to you.

<u>**Call out to God**</u>

God created you so He could love you. He also created you so you could love Him. There is no greater feeling than to experience the love of God and to love Him back with the same intense love He demonstrates for you. Take a moment to reflect on your life experiences and ask yourself, *"Has God been active throughout my life? Do I feel He has truly loved me?"* If you feel He has, talk to him about it. If you feel He has not, ask Him why He has yet to love you. Call out to God today by expressing to Him the thoughts and feelings that arise as you reflect on the love He has shown you, or the love you feel you have yet to receive.

____

____

____

____

____

____

____

____

____

____

____

"For by him all things were created, in heaven and on earth, visible and invisible, whether thrones or dominions or rulers or authorities – all things were created through him and for him."

Colossians 1:16

3

You have rebelled against God

"...for all have sinned and fall short of the glory of God."

Romans 3:23

________________________, recognize that some of your choices in life have turned you away from me. Though I created you to be innocent and holy, you have allowed temptations to persuade you to think and do things that are offensive to me. Because of that, you have separated yourself from me, and you have lost your innocence.

Take a moment to think deeply on God's words to you.

<u>**Call out to God**</u>

In His Word, God says every person has lost his or her innocence. That is, no one is holy as God is holy, therefore God has separated Himself from every person (Isaiah 59:2). We are designed by God *for God*, yet often we think, speak, behave and act in a way that dishonors Him.

Before you call out to God today, pause to reflect on what God is saying to you. God says, **"*All* have sinned and fall short of my glory."** Neither you nor anyone else has lived a sinless life, and neither you nor anyone else has the power to glorify God apart from God. Allow yourself to feel the weight of these words and respond to God by telling Him what you are doing (*or not doing)* that causes you to fall short of His glory.

"...for all have sinned and fall short of the glory of God."

Romans 3:23

4

You are dead in your sin

"Therefore, just as sin came into the world through one man, and death through sin, and so death spread to all men because all have sinned."

Romans 5:12

____

_______________________, you have chosen to manage your life on your own, without me. You still have all I provide for you— your brain, your body, your ability and your will to do whatever you want with your life. However, without your innocence, you cannot enjoy perfect union with me.

____

Take a moment to think deeply on God's words to you.

<u>**Call Out To God**</u>

Each of us has the desire to be fully alive to God, to ourselves and to the world around us. However, in His Word God says, *"everyone who lives apart from me is spiritually dead"* (Ephesians 2:1). He says we are dead in our sin and therefore not alive to Him, to our truest self or the world He created. Therefore naturally, because we are spiritually dead, we fight to feel fully alive by serving all that makes us feel like we are actually living. Some of us attempt to accomplish this by serving ourselves, our families, our careers, our status, our money, sports, entertainment, hobbies, drugs, alcohol or any combination of these and more. The truth is, however, to truly live we must desire and serve God above every other person and thing. We must make knowing and experiencing God the aim of our lives.

Ask yourself: *"Am I willing to desire God above my family, my career, my money, my hobbies and my sin? Am I willing to make knowing and experiencing God the ultimate pursuit of my life?"* God says, "Draw near to me and I will draw near to you" (James 4:8a). He says, **"Ask, and it will be given to you, seek, and you will find; knock, and it will be opened to you" Matthew 7:7.**

Are you willing to draw near to God? If so, express to God your desire to know and experience Him for all that He is and all He is truly worth.

____

____

____

____

"Therefore, just as sin came into the world through one man,
and death through sin, and so death spread to all men
because all have sinned."

Romans 5:12

5

GOD

God is the Creator and Sustainer of all things

"In the beginning, God created the heavens and the earth."

Genesis 1:1

____

"I praise you, for I am fearfully and wonderfully made.

Wonderful are your works; my soul knows it very well."

Psalm 139:14

____

______________________, everything that is beautiful in the world is my creation. I created the heights of the heavens and the depths of the ocean. I created the stars in the sky above you and the flowers and trees on the land beneath you. And you, above all, are my most treasured creation; for you were formed in the image of me.

____

Take a moment to think deeply on God's words to you.

<u>**Call Out To God**</u>

You are experiencing God every moment of every day; there is not a time or place where God is not present and active. As the sun rises above you each morning, God is revealing to you His desire to provide. Likewise, as you use the mind and body God created for you, God is revealing to you His desire to see you prosper and succeed. As you call out to God today, acknowledge Him as the Creator of all things, and express to Him your appreciation for all He provides.

    DAY 5 | GOD IS THE CREATOR AND SUSTAINER OF ALL THINGS

"In the beginning, God created the Heavens and the Earth."

Genesis 1:1

"I praise you, for I am fearfully and wonderfully made.

Wonderful are your works; my soul knows it very well."

Psalm 139:14

6

God is sacred and holy

"There is none holy like the LORD: for there is none besides you; there is no rock like our God."

1 Samuel 2:2

____

_________________________, there is no other God but me and there is no one who is righteous apart from me.

____

Take a moment to think deeply on God's words to you.

<u>**Call out to God**</u>

God is holy. And once you choose to embrace Him and claim Him as your Spiritual Father, you too will be made holy. In His Word, God says, **"Everyone who calls on the name of the Lord will be saved" (Romans 10:13),** and those who are born-again will **"present [themselves] in splendor, without spot or wrinkle or any such thing, that [they] might be holy and without blemish" (Ephesians 5:27).** It is your destiny to be saved—*to be born-again*—and to experience life *with* God. As you call out to God today, express to Him your desire to be holy, and beg Him to restore your innocence so that you present yourself blameless, without blemish and free from accusation on the Day of Judgment.

____

____

____

____

____

____

____

____

____

____

"There is none holy like the LORD: for there is none besides you;

there is no rock like our God."

1 Samuel 2:2

7

God is Love

"For God so loved the world, that he gave his one and only Son,

that whoever believes in him should not perish

but have eternal life."

John 3:16

"...but God shows his love for us in that while we were still sinners,

Christ died for us."

Romans 5:8

______________________, there is nothing you can do that will make me love you more; nor is there anything you can do that will cause me to love you less. I am the essence of love and it is my nature to love you. I love you so much that I came down from heaven to reveal myself and provide for you the opportunity to experience my love forever.

Take a moment to think deeply on God's words to you.

<u>**Call Out To God**</u>

God loves you more than anyone else could ever love you and will ever love you, and He demonstrated His love for you by taking action. God came down from heaven and lived among humanity so you and I would come to know and experience Him for who He truly is. In His Word, God says, **"This is eternal life—that they know Me, the only true God, and Jesus Christ, whom I have sent" John 17:3.** My friend, **Jesus is the pathway to God.** To know and be known by Jesus is your greatest aim and ultimate destiny; there is no greater satisfaction, and no other name is there by which you must be saved. As you call out to God today, ask Him to reveal to you—*Jesus.* Ask God to give you a passion for knowing and experiencing Jesus for who He truly is and all He is truly worth.

____

____

____

____

____

____

____

____

____

"For God so loved the world, that he gave his one and only Son,

that whoever believes in him should not perish

but have eternal life."

John 3:16

"...but God shows his love for us in that while we were still sinners,

Christ died for us."

Romans 5:8

8

JESUS

Jesus is God

"I and the Father are one."

John 10:30

"[Jesus] is the radiance of the glory of God and the exact imprint of his nature, and he upholds the universe by the word of his power."

Hebrews 1:3a

__________________________, even before I created the world, Jesus was with me. Just as I have always been, He has always been. We never had a beginning and we will never grow out of being. Jesus and I are one in the same.

Take a moment to think deeply on God's words to you.

<u>**Call Out To God**</u>

Jesus is God in human form. He lives as God lives and does as God does. While on earth, there is nothing Jesus did that God does not do, and there is nothing Jesus left undone. Jesus healed the sick and gave sight to the blind. He displayed mercy and stood for justice. He offered grace and loved in action. Jesus changed the world. He started with 12 followers and now has more than 2 billion people acknowledging Him as Savior and Lord.

Are you willing to admit your need for a Savior and allow Jesus to transform your life? Consider your conversations with God and your life experiences these past seven days. *Is God revealing Himself to you? Are you beginning to desire Him? Are you experiencing God's call on your life?*

Pour your heart out to Jesus today. Share with Him your intimate thoughts, feelings and emotions. Tell Jesus why you need Him and why you do not want to go on living your life without knowing and being known by Him.

____

____

____

____

____

____

____

"I and the Father are one."

John 10:30

"[Jesus] is the radiance of the glory of God and the exact imprint of his nature, and he upholds the universe by the word of his power."

Hebrews 1:3a

9

Jesus has the power to save sinners

"He himself bore our sins in his body on the tree, that

we might die to sin and live to righteousness.

By his wounds you have been healed."

1 Peter 2:24

"And there is salvation in no one else, for there is no other name

under heaven given among men by which we must be saved."

Romans 3:25

"Repent therefore, and turn back, that your sins may be blotted out,

that times of refreshing may come from the presence of the Lord,

and that he may send the Christ appointed for you."

Acts 3:19-20

________________________________, my Son revealed to the world exactly what it means to truly live, and in doing so, He was condemned and sentenced to die. He willingly gave His life to save yours. If you will receive my Son by putting your faith and trust in Him,

repenting of your sin and desiring Him above every other venture
you pursue, you will be saved.

Take a moment to think deeply on God's words to you.

<u>**Call Out To God**</u>

Jesus alone has the power to connect you to God. If you desire God,
you must first desire Jesus. God sent Jesus to earth to reveal to the
world the true love of God. In His Word, God says**, "Greater love has
no one than this, that someone lay down his life for his friends"
John 15:13.** Pause for a moment to recognize that this is exactly what
Jesus did for you. He demonstrated for you the love of God by
becoming sin and sacrificing His life so you might believe in Him and
be reconciled to God. During His earthly life, Jesus said—

***"I am the way, and the truth, and the life. No one comes to the
Father except through me" John 14:6.***

*Will you choose to believe in Jesus? Will you choose to believe Jesus is
the Son of God and that He died on a cross to save you?   Will you
surrender your sins at the cross of Christ, repent from what you know
to be evil, and beg Jesus to forgive you and save you?*
If so, in your own words, ask Him to.

"He himself bore our sins in his body on the tree, that

we might die to sin and live to righteousness.

By his wounds you have been healed."

1 Peter 2:24

"And there is salvation in no one else, for there is no other name

under heaven given among men by which we must be saved."

Romans 3:25

Repent therefore, and turn back, that your sins may be blotted out,

that times of refreshing may come from the presence of the Lord,

and that he may send the Christ appointed for you."

Acts 3:19-20

10

Jesus defeated death

"Yet a little while and the world will see me no more, but you will see me. Because I live, you also will live. In that day you will know that I am in my Father, and you in me, and I in you."

John 14:19-20

"[Jesus] was delivered up for our trespasses and raised for our justification."

Romans 4:25

________________________, Jesus is alive and united with me in heaven. He died an earthly death only to rise to eternal life. Likewise, everyone who despises their sin and turns from it and believes in Jesus' life, death and resurrection, they too will be united with me in heaven.

Take a moment to think deeply on God's words to you.

<u>**TALK TO JESUS**</u>

When you receive Jesus as God; as the forgiver of your sins; as Lord of your life; as your utmost satisfaction; as your ultimate pursuit; and as the One whom you desire to honor and emulate the rest of your life, then you will be saved and inherit eternal life.

Have you chosen to receive Jesus in this manner? Have you chosen to receive Jesus for who He truly is? Jesus says, **"If anyone would come after me, let him deny himself and take up his cross and follow me. For whoever would save his life will lose it, but whoever loses his life for my sake will find it" Matthew 16:24-25.**

Are you willing to follow Jesus wherever He leads you? Are you willing to deny yourself in order to magnify God and make Jesus known to the people around you?

If your heart's response to these questions is "yes", then rejoice! According to God's Word, your sinful heart has been removed and a new heart—*the heart of Christ*—is alive within you. By God's own authority, you are born-again and because Jesus lives, you live! As you TALK TO JESUS today, praise Him for saving you and reuniting you with your heavenly Father.

If your heart's response is "no", I encourage you to continue calling out to God, asking Him to reveal to you the truth about Jesus.

Through His Word, God says to you, *"If you confess with your mouth that Jesus is Lord, believe in your heart that I raised him from the dead, and keep the commandments set forth by My Son, you will be saved" (Romans 10:9; John 3:36).*

"Yet a little while and the world will see me no more, but you will see me. Because I live, you also will live. In that day you will know that I am in my Father, and you in me, and I in you."

John 14:19-20

"[Jesus] was delivered up for our trespasses

and raised for our justification."

Romans 4:25

11

Jesus is the mediator between God and you

**"I am writing these things to you so that you may not sin.
But if anyone does sin, we have an advocate with the Father,
Jesus Christ, the righteous."**

1 John 2:1

**"...he is able to save to the uttermost those who draw near to God
through him, since he always lives to make intercession for them."**

Hebrews 7:25

_______________________, Jesus sits at my right hand and mediates as your Advocate and High Priest. He is the mediator between me and every person who has been made new. It is through Him alone that your prayers are heard and answered.

Take a moment to think deeply on God's words to you.

<u>**TALK TO JESUS**</u>

If you have received Jesus for who He truly is, you have been born-again. Your sins have been forgiven and you have regained your innocence. God no longer sees your sin; He sees only the righteousness of Christ living inside you. The moment you received Jesus, you received an Advocate. Jesus is your Advocate and High Priest, and through Him, you have gained direct access to God. Having Jesus as your Advocate means not one of your prayers goes unheard. **Your prayers have the power of Christ in them!** You are free to speak to God anytime and anywhere and you have the ability to hear His voice. *What will you say to Him?*

Christian, enjoy this amazing favor and TALK TO JESUS!

"I am writing these things to you so that you may not sin. But if anyone does sin, we have an advocate with the Father, Jesus Christ, the righteous."

1 John 2:1

"...he is able to save to the uttermost those who draw near to God through him, since he always lives to make intercession for them."

Hebrews 7:25

12

HOLY SPIRIT

"God's love has been poured into our hearts through the Holy Spirit

who has been given to us."

Romans 5:5b

"The Holy Spirit lives in every believer upon salvation and it is the

believer's responsibility to be controlled by the Holy Spirit."

(Romans 8:9-11; Ephesians 5:18; 1 John 2:20,27)

________________________, upon receiving my Son, you have also received my Spirit to guide you, bless you and bring you into perfect union with my Son and me. Holy Spirit will reveal to you my divine purpose as He fills you with righteousness and draws you closer to me. He will convict you of every sin and empower you to live an honorable life. He will teach you truths that the world cannot teach as He enables you to adopt my wisdom and understanding. He will be with you always—empowering you, strengthening you and assuring you of your salvation.

Take a moment to think deeply on God's words to you.

TALK TO JESUS

Holy Spirit is the Divine Person of God who lives inside of every born-again person. The Holy Spirit makes the miracle of your new birth possible. In His Word God says**, "And I will give you a new heart, and a new spirit I will put within you. And I will remove the heart of stone from your flesh and give you a heart of flesh. And I will put my Spirit within you, and cause you to walk in my statutes and be careful to obey my rules" Ezekiel 36:26-27.**

If you have received Jesus, Holy Spirit is already working to remove from within you everything that is not of God while simultaneously filling you with everything God is. The attributes which characterize the Holy Spirit are **"love, joy, peace, patience, kindness, goodness, faithfulness, gentleness and self-control" (Galatians 5:22-23),** and His attributes manifest within you as you call on Him to fill you. Holy Spirit is your Comfort, your Strength, your Counselor and your Helper. He will never leave or forsake you, and daily He will remind you of everything God is, does and desires.

As you pray today, acknowledge the Holy Spirit's indwelling presence in your life. Call on Holy Spirit by name and ask Him to fill you with His own attributes. Allow yourself to feel the love, joy, peace, patience, kindness, goodness, faithfulness and gentleness of God as you speak to the Spirit of God who now resides in your new heart.

"God's love has been poured into our hearts through the Holy Spirit

who has been given to us."

Romans 5:5b

"The Holy Spirit lives in every believer upon salvation and it is the

believer's responsibility to be controlled by the Holy Spirit."

(Romans 8:9-11; Ephesians 5:18; 1 John 2:20,27)

13

THE WORD OF GOD

"All scripture is breathed out by God and profitable for teaching, for reproof, for correction, and for training in righteousness, that the man of God may be complete, equipped for every good work."
2 Timothy 3:16-17

"For the Word of God is living and active, sharper than any two-edged sword, piercing to the division of the soul and of spirit, of joints and of marrow, and discerning the thoughts and intentions of the heart." Hebrews 4:12

**"Your word is a lamp to my feet and a light to my path.
Your word is truth." Psalm 119:105; John 17:17b**

_______________________, I live through my Word and manifest myself to you through your interaction with it. As you absorb my Word into your mind, I will renew your way of thinking and transform the way you feel, speak, behave and act.

Every word I have spoken is alive and active and filled with my

power. Avail yourself to my Word. Abide in it and live from it,

and you will be satisfied.

Take a moment to think deeply on God's words to you.

TALK TO JESUS

God is found in His Word. You cannot experience the fullness of God without experiencing Him through His Word. God says, **"Be attentive to my words; incline your ear to my sayings. Let them not escape from your sight; keep them within your heart. For they are life to those who find them, and healing to all their flesh" Proverbs 4:20-22.** To experience God's Word means to abide in it and live from it, to absorb it into your mind until it transforms the way you think, feel, speak, behave and act.

If you do not yet have a Bible, be encouraged to get one. A variety of Bibles are available for you to choose from at any Christian bookstore. There is also a unique app entitled "The Bible App" by Life.Church that you can upload for free in your app store. As you pray today, ask God to give you a passion for reading, receiving and responding to His Word. Ask God to reveal Himself to you and manifest Himself within you as you absorb His Word into your mind and into your heart.

____

____

____

____

____

____

____

____

"All scripture is breathed out by God and profitable for teaching, for reproof, for correction, and for training in righteousness, that the man of God may be complete, equipped for every good work."
2 Timothy 3:16-17

"For the Word of God is living and active, sharper than any two-edged sword, piercing to the division of the soul and of spirit, of joints and of marrow, and discerning the thoughts and intentions of the heart." **Hebrews 4:12**

"Your word is a lamp to my feet and a light to my path. Your word is truth." **Psalm 119:105; John 17:17b**

14

THE CHURCH

"...so we, though many, are one in the body of Christ, and individual members of one another."

Romans 12:5

"A new commandment I give to you, that you love one another: just as I have loved you, you also are to love one another."

John 13:34

_________________________, the moment you received Jesus, you were born into my family and my body of believers. Together with members of my family, you will be my hands and feet bringing hope to the world. It is my greatest delight to see my family worship together, pray together and enjoy life together.

Take a moment to think deeply on God's words to you.

God calls you to commit to a local church body. He wills that you join with fellow believers in hearing the Word of God preached, and He desires for you to commit to loving and admonishing fellow believers in the truth you were born into. In His Word God says, **"...love one another: just as I have loved you, you also are to love one another. By this everyone will know that you are my disciples, if you love one another" John 13:34-35.** Christian, God desires for you to love and be loved by His local church. God's local church is simply a community of believers who are committed to sharing the love of Christ with each other and the community and city they serve. As you pray today, ask God to lead you to a local church body who will benefit from the talents and gifts God gives you. Likewise, ask God to lead you to a body of believers who will love and encourage you as you grow in likeness to Jesus.

____

____

____

____

____

____

____

____

____

____

"…so we, though many, are one in the body of Christ, and individual members of one another."

Romans 12:5

"A new commandment I give to you, that you love one another: just as I have loved you, you also are to love one another."

John 13:34

Take action on your prayer today by seeking and committing to a local church family with whom you honor God by loving one another and enacting the works of Christ.

RECEIVE JESUS

Have you made the commitment to receive Jesus for who He truly is? Have you begun to fellowship with God and experience the joy of knowing and being known by Jesus? If so, the remainder of this book is written for you. You are now moments away from illuminating your prayer life and experiencing the fullness of God. Prayer is your pathway to knowing God and following His will, and the 40 Day Journey that follows will teach you how to pray so that every moment of your life you are in an attitude of relationship to Jesus. May God richly bless you on this journey as He empowers you with the ministry of prayer. For an overview of the 40 Day Journey, refer to pages 1-4 titled **INTRODUCTION.**

Important: To truly experience Jesus for all that He is, commit to exploring your 40 Day Journey one day at a time – as each day prepares you for the next. Your 40 Day Journey can be experienced alone, with a partner or in a group setting. Before you begin, consider which experience works best for you.

As you embark on this journey, it is important to know where your journey leads and where your journey ends. In a time in which humanity has given themselves over to everything *but* prayer, this journey paves the way back to prayer and ultimately back to God. Be encouraged from your journey's beginning to *let go* of every fruitless activity. Rid your life of empty distractions and free yourself from the ways of the world by giving yourself completely to God and to prayer. Determine to pour your heart and soul into your prayers until you experience the joyous satisfaction that arises as you TALK TO JESUS.

QR Codes – The 40 Day Journey contains QR codes that link to more than 25 exclusive 1-5-minute video introductions.

Begin each day by scanning the code to receive additional insights designed to encourage, empower and prepare you for each of your daily readings.

WHY PRAY?

Prayer causes things to happen

"You do not have, because you do not ask." James 4:2b

A prayer for you today

Jesus, help us see how our prayers activate your power to carry out your will. Teach and inspire us with your Word as you prepare our hearts and minds to receive from you a revelation. It is in your name we pray, Amen.

Are there things about you that you would like to change? Are there circumstances you find yourself in that you desire to make different? The most substantial resource you have at your disposal to change any situation in your life or in the lives of others is prayer. Nothing you do, be it planning, strategizing or complete

Your prayers activate God's power to do the unimaginable

My Personal Revelations

____

____

____

____

____

____

____

____

____

____

____

____

71

implementation will be of greater influence or have a more significant impact than prayer. *Why?*

Two related reasons:

1. With man some things are possible, but with God *all* things are possible.

2. "Prayer causes things to happen that would not happen if you did not pray."

– John Piper, American pastor, author and founder of desiringGod.org

Before you begin to change anything, you should plead with God to act on behalf of that which you seek to change. *Would you rather work at changing something on your own, or would you rather work at changing something together with God? Who would you rather have in charge of changing something—yourself or God?*

Prayer is designed for you to communicate with God so that you remain near to Him. Through prayer God invites you to call on Him because He wants to make a difference for you and for everyone—*for the better.*

72

Jesus' disciples knew the power and the importance of prayer. The twelve disciples walked through life with the most influential person who ever lived, and because of their proximity to Jesus, they changed the world. It is amazing to note that while with Jesus, "the twelve disciples heard the greatest sermon ever preached, yet never asked Jesus to teach them *how to preach*. The disciples witnessed the greatest healer to ever heal, yet never asked Jesus to teach them to do miracles. The twelve disciples did, however, ask Jesus to teach them *how to pray*" [1] because they knew if they wanted to be as influential as Jesus was, they needed to pray as Jesus prayed.

On the authority of God's Word, know this: If you open yourself up to the teachings in this book and begin to employ that which you learn, your prayers will change your life. Your prayers will affect everything in you and around you in ways you have not imagined.

Your prayers will change your world.

> *"You do not have because you do not ask."*
> *James 4:2b*

<u>**A Talk To Jesus Testimony**</u>

"I remember the first time I called out to God. I was seventeen years old and utterly depressed, kneeling in my childhood basement underneath a pull-up bar my dad had hung for my brother and me. During this time in my life, living was no longer a pleasure or adventure; it had become a burden and a losing battle. During much of my adolescence, I struggled to fight against anxiety and depression. The anxiety and depression I faced had such a tight grip on my life that it felt nearly inescapable. It was severe and debilitating, and in this moment, it had brought me to my knees and caused me to call out to God.

As I knelt beneath that pull-up bar clinching the jump rope I intended to hang myself with, the latter portion of one thought would prevent me from suicide and ultimately steer me onto a path that led to God. On the brink of suicide kneeling in my parent's basement, I

74

thought, 'I don't want to live, *but I am too scared to die.*

As this thought echoed in my mind, I got up from the basement floor and walked back upstairs to my bedroom. Lying there with my face covered in tears I spoke to God for the first time. I said to Him, "God, I don't want to live, but I am too scared to die."

Having never spoken to God before, this single spark of communication from me to Him awakened me to the possibility of hope. Likewise, according to God's Word, this single spark of communication from me to Him activated His power to draw me to Himself and change the direction of my life.

I did not experience salvation in this moment, however. I was not convicted of any sins I had committed nor was I repentant of any behavior or actions I was engaging in. Nevertheless, the hope I felt would not go away. The hope I received on this night would gradually propel me toward understanding the Gospel and receiving the Christ with whom I never intended to have a relationship.

My prayer, as simple as it was, caused things to happen in my life that would not have happened if I did not pray. And that simple spark of communication that occurred under that pull-up bar continues to generate hope and change in me and through me to this day."

Taking Action

For today's Taking Action, think back to a time (or the first time) you called out to God and He answered your prayer. *How did you feel? What was your situation or circumstance?* Allow yourself time to reflect on this moment of calling out to God, and let it give you confidence knowing that prayer causes things to happen that would not happen if you did not pray.

[1] Sermon excerpt: "Lord, Teach Us To Pray" by Leonard Ravenhill, an English Christian evangelist known for his life of prayer

<u>Day One</u>

Taking Action

Reflect upon a time (or the first time) you called out to God and He answered your prayer. Allow your remembrance of this moment to give you confidence knowing that your prayers cause things to happen that would not happen if you did not pray.
Writing space is available for you below and on the following page.

78

God governs the world through His Word and the prayers of His people

"Man shall not live by bread alone, but by every word that comes from the mouth of God."

Matthew 4:4

"And this is the confidence that we have toward Him, that if we ask anything according to his will, he hears us. And if we know that he hears us in whatever we ask, we know that we have the requests that we have asked of him."

1 John 5:14-15

A prayer for you today

Jesus, we call on you to reveal your will for our lives today and each day going

Seek, find, and follow God's will for your life; make it count!

My Personal Revelations

forward. We acknowledge that your will is found in your Word, and we trust you to speak to us through it. We are dependent on you, Lord, and long to be in contact with you so that by our fruit you receive glory. Hear our hearts as we pray, and speak to us as we read and engage with you. Amen.

Be encouraged to seek, find, and follow God's will for your life; make it count! In no other way will you fulfill your destiny than by living your life following the will of God, and in no other way will God be more satisfied in you.

To follow God's will is simply to desire what God desires and do what pleases Him. Since the only way to know what pleases God is to know and experience Him, and the only way to know and experience God is through prayer and your dependency on His Word—prayer and the Word of God must reside in you richly.

God speaks to you through His Word, and you respond to Him with prayer. Likewise, you speak to God, and He responds to you through His Word. Prayer and the Word of God are inseparably joined and are essential to knowing God and following His will. Only when you read the Word of God, absorb it and allow it to penetrate the core of who you are, will you be able to carry out the perfect will of God. Believer, as you venture through these 40 days of fellowship with God, you will seek, find and follow God's will for your life. You will find yourself enjoying what God enjoys as you delight in Him and acquire a newly found reverence for His Word. Be encouraged from this day forward, to welcome scripture into your mind, heart and emotions and to allow it to take over. As you hear and feel God speaking to you through His Word, simply listen, and follow His voice.

"Man shall not live by bread alone, but by every word that comes from the mouth of God." Matthew 4:4

<u>Taking Action</u>

Prayer and the Word of God work together to enable you to experience the fullness of God, and for this reason, more than 120 passages of scripture fill the pages of this 40 Day Journey.

Today's Taking Action is a jumpstart to an exercise you are encouraged to engage in throughout the entirety of your 40 days. Beginning today, allow yourself to experience each scripture you read. That is, rather than simply reading a passage of scripture quickly and moving on to the next, allow yourself to *feel* what God is saying to you. **Let the Word of God speak into your mind until the mind of God transforms your heart!**

Do not forget to jot down your thoughts and feelings in *My Personal Revelations.*

82

<u>Day 2</u>

Taking Action

Absorb God's Word into your mind today by slowly reading each passage of scripture (perhaps rereading each passage a few times) to experience the message God is conveying to you.

<u>Today's Scriptures</u>

"Man shall not live by bread alone, but by every word that comes from the mouth of God."

Matthew 4:4

"And this is the confidence that we have toward Him, that if we ask anything according to His will, he hears us. And if we know that He hears us in whatever we ask, we know that we have the requests that we have asked of Him."

1 John 5:14-15

Consider using the writing space provided in *My Personal Revelations* to express the thoughts and feelings that arise as the fruit of your scripture meditation.

I encourage you to continue this action throughout the 40 days!

God uses prayer to change us

"I will give you a new heart and a new spirit I will put within you. And I will remove the heart of stone from your flesh and give you a heart of flesh. And I will put my Spirit within you, and cause you to walk in my statutes."
Ezekiel 36:26-27

"But the fruit of the Spirit is love, joy, peace, patience, kindness, goodness, faithfulness, gentleness, and self-control." Galatians 5:22-23

A prayer for you today

Jesus, it is our greatest desire to have changed hearts, so we might emulate you with our lives. Together with my friend in Christ, we thank you for sending us a

If you desire to change, pray, because prayer is the catalyst for change

My Personal Revelations

____
____
____
____
____
____
____
____
____
____
____
____
____

84

Helper who can transform us into your likeness. Anoint us with your Holy Spirit and fill us with His attributes. See to it that we submit to His leadership and follow His counsel. Transform us for your glory alone. Amen.

If you desire to change, pray, because prayer is the catalyst for change. Prayer is God's gift to you that you can open all the time, anytime and anywhere. Solely through prayer do you gain access to God and invite Him in to construct spiritual transformation. Spiritual transformation is the innermost change of your mind which then renews the condition of your heart, whereby enabling you to "discern the will of God and do what is good and acceptable and perfect" (Romans 12:2b). Spiritual transformation cannot take place without God or the Spirit of God who lives within you. For transformation to occur, a Christ-induced change must happen at the deepest level of your mind so that your heart's attitude conforms to the

"Do not conform to the pattern of this world, but be transformed by the renewal of your mind."
Romans 12:2a

heart-attitude of Jesus. To experience transformation, all that is in you that has been conformed to the world and is of a worldly perspective must be repented of and a Spirit-led, Godly perspective must be born in its place.

Consider for a moment God's interpreted word spoken to you through Romans 8:7-10. In it, God says to you, *"your human mind is hostile to me and therefore cannot submit to my will; only a mind that is controlled and transformed by the indwelling Spirit is able to render my will."* Believer, if you choose to live by the will of your mind, you will oppose the will of God. However, as you seek to renew your mind by feeding into it the Word of God and praying for a filling of the Holy Spirit, you will attune to the perfect will of God. From this day forward, determine to incline your heart and mind to the heart and mind of God until **what you enjoy doing is what God desires for you to do.** In this, there is no greater transformation,

86

and there is no greater resemblance of God's will being active in your life.

Taking Action

As you prepare for transformation through the Holy Spirit, it is important to know who the Holy Spirit is. Holy Spirit is the Person of God who lives within you, and He is the only Person capable of transforming you into the perfect image of Jesus. His attributes are **love, joy, peace, patience, kindness, goodness, faithfulness, gentleness and self-control**, and He enriches you with His attributes as you call on Him to do so. For the first part of today's Taking Action, you are invited to identify one of the nine attributes of the Holy Spirit that you would like to pray for and grow in throughout these 40 days. Be encouraged to choose the one attribute of the Spirit that you feel needs the most enrichment in your life. For the second part of today's Taking Action, you are invited to choose one person in your life (a family member, a friend or someone else) whom you would like to pray for throughout these 40 days. Your purpose for praying for this person can be anything.

For example:

- *Would you like this person to experience salvation?*

- *Would you like this person to receive a greater measure of any of the nine characteristics of the Holy Spirit?*

Choose one person and one purpose for praying.

Note → As you pray to be filled by the Holy Spirit, be encouraged to accompany your prayer with God's Word. The following link/QR code will direct you to a webpage that enables you to *find out what the Bible says about* the attribute you choose. Consider returning to this site throughout your journey to receive God's Word relative to the attribute you seek.

<u>Day 3</u>

Taking Action

Choose one of the nine attributes of the Holy Spirit that you desire to be filled with and transformed by throughout these 40 days.

Attribute of the Spirit (see page 87):

____

Why did you choose this particular attribute?

____

____

____

Choose one person for whom you will intentionally pray and a specific purpose for praying.

Person I will intentionally pray for:

____

My purpose for praying:

____

____

____

Keep this attribute and person in mind today as you prepare yourself to intentionally pray for them beginning tomorrow.

4

God wants us to pray

"Call to me and I will answer you and will tell you great and hidden things that you have not known."
Jeremiah 33:3

"If my people who are called by my name humble themselves, and pray and seek my face and turn from their wicked ways, then I will hear from heaven and will forgive their sin and heal their land."
2 Chronicles 7:14

A prayer for you today

Jesus, you are more passionate about your relationship with us than you are about every other desire you have. Therefore, we plead with you to

God delights in seeing you transformed and becoming more like Him

My Personal Revelations

produce within us a longing to be in constant communication with you. Fill us with a strong desire to pray and an eagerness to seek your guidance. See to it that we never lose sight of you and never cease to keep you on the forefront of our minds. We thank you for the gift of prayer, and we long to glorify you with it. Amen.

Christian, God delights in seeing you transformed and becoming more like Him. God adores His relationship with you, and He craves the communication that strengthens the relationship. Not one of your prayers goes unheard and not one of your prayers is ever wasted. Take pleasure in knowing that your prayers are being stored in heaven and will one day be poured out onto all the earth! Only through prayer (and the Word of God) are you fortunate to feed into and feed from the source of your existence. Through prayer, you have the opportunity to take part in and have

"Call to me and I will answer you and will tell you great and hidden things that you have not known." Jeremiah 33:3

a say in God's unfolding plan for your life and all of creation!

Can you feel the weight of that?

How greatly might you affect your life through prayer? How greatly might you affect the future of the world when your prayers, in all their power, are one day lavished upon the earth, transforming the landscape of all creation?

Prayer, with all its influence and wonder, ought to be your most treasured experience and favorite adventure! Prayer ought to take precedence over, and fill you with more joy than you receive from everything else you do! Be challenged, believer, to let prayer be the way you begin and end everything. Refuse to leave Jesus behind or move Him to the side. Begin with Him, end with Him, and convey your heart to Him through every activity. Let the love and loyalty of Jesus become the provocation that excites you to pray over, in and through everything you do.

92

<u>Taking Action</u>

It is time to begin talking to Jesus. For today's Taking Action, I invite you to choose a specific place and time in which you intend to pray for at least ten minutes per day each day going forward.

During these ten minutes of uninterrupted prayer, commit to praying for the person and spiritual attribute you chose on Day 3.
Plead with God on this person's behalf, and seek God for opportunities to practice and grow the attribute of the Holy Spirit with which you desire to be filled.

Note → Ten minutes of uninterrupted prayer can seem like hours for some people. If this applies to you, consider splitting your ten minutes of prayer time into two or three prayer sessions.
Example: morning, afternoon, evening

Day 4 I Taking Action on following page

<u>Day 4</u>

Taking Action

Make an appointment with God

Choose a specific place and time in which you intend to speak to God on behalf of the person and spiritual attribute you chose on Day 3. Be sure to choose a place where you will not be distracted and a time in which you can give God your absolute best for at least ten minutes.

Time:

____

Place:

____

Begin talking to Jesus today!

Commit to meeting with God at this specific time and location throughout the remainder of these 40 days. You will be encouraged to increase your prayer time over the course of your 40 Day Journey.

5

<u>God instructs us to pray</u>

"Do not be anxious about anything, but in everything by prayer and supplication with thanksgiving, let your requests be made known to God."
Philippians 4:6

"Pray without ceasing."
1 Thessalonians 5:17

A prayer for you today

Jesus, your holiness inspires us to pray. Your faithfulness entices us to pray. And your Word instructs us to pray. We thank you for the opportunity to speak to and hear from you anytime and all the time. Hear our hearts as we continue to draw close to you through prayer. We pray in your name, Amen.

Living out God's will and becoming like Christ happens through endless fellowship and communication with Him

---

My Personal Revelations

God instructs you to pray for your own good. God knew that for you to experience the fullness of who He is, you must have access to Him always. Therefore, God created prayer.

God wills for you to engage in prayer, live from it, rest in it, and act on it.

You are designed *by God* to live in constant communion *with God.* You cannot succeed in fulfilling God's will without God, and you cannot become like Christ without Christ. Living out God's will and becoming like Christ happens through endless fellowship and communication with Him.

Taking Action

You have accomplished much in 5 days! You are exploring God's Word for all that it is. You have committed to praying for the enrichment of one of the nine attributes of Holy Spirit, and you are intentionally praying for another person. As you continue with your commitments, today's Taking Action provides a well-deserved prayer of encouragement. As we join together in prayer, let us thank God for what He is doing in you and through you and ask Him to inspire you throughout the entirety of your 40 Day Journey!

After praying, you will be introduced to the Three Pillars of Prayer.

<u>Day 5</u>

Taking Action

Please join in prayer

Jesus, we call on you on behalf of our self and others who have chosen to relate with you through the insights and action invitations written in this book. Guard our hearts and minds as you feed into it wisdom and truth. Meet with us as we call out to you with an eagerness to receive empowerment from your Holy Spirit. Likewise, answer our prayers as we advocate on behalf of the people for whom we have chosen to pray. Together, we thank you for the wisdom you have imparted to us thus far, and we ask for continual growth throughout the remainder of these 40 days. We trust you to fulfill your good purpose in our lives. In everything, see to it that you receive glory. Through you we pray, Amen.

CREATING CONSISTENCY

Three actions are essential to creating consistency in prayer. First, you must view prayer as a relationship rather than an obligation or duty. Second, you must make the commitment to speak to and hear from God. Third, you must have a well-balanced prayer life.

The Three Pillars of Prayer are

Relationship • Commitment • Balance

PRAYER

RELATIONSHIP	COMMITMENT	BALANCE

Prayer is a relationship with God

"Draw near to God and he will draw near to you." James 4:8

Demonstrate your love for God by giving Him your quality time

A prayer for you today

Jesus, it is a blessing to live life with the joy and peace of knowing you. There is no greater joy than to know you and be known by you, and there is no greater honor than to glorify you by living according to your Word. Inspire us to draw closer to you, and as we do, draw closer to us. We ask and pray in your holy name, Amen.

Having a healthy relationship with God requires the same energy and effort necessary to grow and sustain any healthy relationship. God created

My Personal Revelations

relationships and desires for every relationship you engage in to be healthy, *especially your relationship with Him!* Regarding your relationship with God, let it be your ambition to give Him your *Quality Time, Respect, Spontaneity and Trust (QRST).*

Quality Time

Time is perhaps the most valuable resource you possess, whereas without it you could do nothing. Furthermore, the way you choose to spend your time often defines your passions and lifetime goals and aspirations.

For example, you choose to spend time studying because you aspire to be educated. Likewise, you choose to spend time working because you aspire to demonstrate your talents and skill while making money. This same analogy applies to your relationship with God. You choose to spend quality time with God because you aspire to have a healthy relationship with Him.

Christian, as you pursue God, you must recognize that there is no better way to spend your time than by spending it in communication with Him.

Quality Time is your treasured meeting with God comprised of uninterrupted prayer and careful meditation on His Word. I encourage you, and God begs of you, to demonstrate the desire you have for Him by giving Him your most valuable resource: your quality time.

Respect

Obedience to God's Word is the foundation to a powerful prayer life. Without obedience to God's Word, you will not enjoy close fellowship with God. When you say to God "I love you" with words, yet refuse to honor Him by *keeping His Word*, you send God mixed signals and deceive only yourself. However, when you respect God by responding to His Word with obedience, you reaffirm the words of praise you speak to Him.

"Draw near to God and he will draw near to you."
James 4:8

Believer, understand that the Word of God was written to convey to you—*God!* God is found in His Word and manifests Himself through you by way of your obedience *to* His Word. Before going any further in your 40 Day Journey, you must understand and acknowledge that your level of intimacy with God, and the joy which follows, is measured by the admiration and respect you have for keeping His Word.

Spontaneity

What makes relationships so great is their sense of surprise. Relationships thrive on spontaneity as it creates excitement and wonder while inducing joy and hope.

Your prayer life is not meant to be ritualistic but rather filled with spontaneity. Spontaneous prayers keep your prayer life fresh and somewhat unpredictable, therefore you should never resist the urge to pray!

In addition to enjoying uninterrupted

102

quality time with God, speak to Him throughout the day by conversing with Him in an unplanned, naturally impulsive manner. In doing so, your relationship with God will continue to generate excitement and growth, and intimacy with Him will manifest itself genuinely and profoundly.

Trust

Allowing yourself to rely on the integrity and faithfulness of God produces within you a spirit of confidence and peace. Your commitment to stay loyal to God and His commitment to remain trustworthy to you is pivotal for your maturity and growth. Thankfully, God's Word says, **"Jesus Christ is the same yesterday and today and forever"** **(Hebrews 13:8).**
Your God is unchanging. His love is enduring, and His patience is unfading. He is unfailingly trustworthy, and He is worthy to receive your unwavering trust.

<u>**Taking Action**</u>

Having a healthy relationship with God is essential to knowing God and following His will for your life. For today's Taking Action, be encouraged to think deeply upon all that is written in Day 6. Take time to review today's message as you consider committing the QRST acronym to memory. Be sure to pull out insights that speak to your heart and write about them in *My Personal Revelations.*

<u>Day 6</u>

Taking Action

Consider reviewing today's message.

Allow key insights to resonate in your mind and affect your heart.

Questions you might consider as you reflect on today's reading:

- *Has my ten minutes of prayer per day been Quality Time?*
- *Am I absorbing God's Word well enough so that it does its job of producing within me an eternal perspective?*
- *Am I in an attitude of relationship to Jesus every moment of every day?*

Jot down your thoughts and feelings in *My Personal Revelations.*

Prayer calls for commitment

"Rejoice always, pray without ceasing, give thanks in all circumstances; for this is the will of God in Christ Jesus for you." 1 Thessalonians 5:16-18

A prayer for you

Jesus, we are motivated to love you because you first loved us. When you chose to die on a cross while we were yet sinners, you revealed to us and to the world your commitment to remain faithful. Let this love you demonstrated breed within us the will to commit our lives to you. Give my friend in Christ and me a passion for prayer and a desire to commit to communing with you each moment of our lives. We pray these things in your name, Amen.

The busyness of life will always deter you from praying unless you make it a priority

---

My Personal Revelations

105

A commitment is a wholehearted determination to bring to pass that which you have pledged to remain faithful to, and when you received Jesus, you entered into a covenant relationship that calls for a lifetime commitment. As you seek to remain faithfully committed to God, it is important for you to realize that your commitment to God is only as strong as your commitment to receiving His Word and communicating with Him through prayer.

With this in mind, prayer must not be viewed simply as random erratic conversations with God spurred by your sudden cravings for Him. Rather, prayer requires a commitment to spending uninterrupted quality time with God, filled with deep-hearted conversation and careful meditation on His Word.

Without an absolute commitment to prayer, you will be vulnerable to—

106

The Devil's Distraction

Intimacy with the Father cultivates through quality time spent alone with Him. There is nothing Satan despises more than your quality time alone with God, and he will try his best to distract you from it. For this reason, it is important for you to be intentional when choosing to spend quality time with God. Each day you must *plan to pray* by identifying a specific place and time that you set aside to do nothing other than speak to and hear from the Lord. You must be sure to choose a place and time where and when distractions are limited, if not completely avoided.

Your Flesh's Resistance

Prayer is often resisted for three reasons:

Excuse – You tell yourself you do not have time.

The busyness of life will always deter you from praying unless you make it a priority.

107

Control – You feel you can rely on your human strength to accomplish God's will rather than relying solely on Him. *The confidence you have in yourself will hinder your dependency on God and keep you from following His will.*

Disbelief – You do not believe prayer makes any or enough difference to warrant your time and effort. *Your inactive prayer life feeds your disbelief and your disbelief responds by not praying. Never resist the urge to pray.*

Relying on Human Strength

God created you and provides for your every need; it is not the other way around. When you finally realize you are only as strong as your dependency on God, then and only then will you commit yourself to praying and treasure prayer above every other activity. Prayer is a supernatural experience that activates a Supernatural Power capable of

"Rejoice always, pray without ceasing, give thanks in all circumstances; for this is the will of God in Christ Jesus for you."
1 Thessalonians 5:16-18

producing supernatural results.
No one can do what God can do
through a person who has committed
himself or herself to prayer.

Taking Action

Before you commit to praying, you
must have a desire to pray or the
commitment will not last. For today's
Taking Action, ask yourself, *"What is it
that causes me to want to commit to
praying to God?"*
Your cause for praying often derives
from one, two or all three of these
reasons:

1. God has proven Himself trustworthy
    and worthy of your commitment to
    pray.

2. Your love for God and God's love for
    you assures that your commitment
    to pray will be a longing pleasure
    and an adventurous experience.

3. You have an absolute dependency
    on God. You rely on Him to remain

faithful and prayer ensures that you stay connected to Him always.

Which of these reasons inspires you to pray? Is it because God is trustworthy? Is it because you love Him? Is it because He is your reason for hope?

For today's Taking Action, express to God your desire to pray by acknowledging the reason(s) why you are choosing to spend your quality time speaking to and hearing from Him.

DAY 7 | PRAYER CALLS FOR COMMITMENT

Taking Action

My Commitment to Pray

God, you have proven yourself trustworthy and worthy of my commitment to pray. For this reason, I will make speaking to and hearing from you the main priority of my life.

Signed

God, my love for you and your love for me *is* my cause for praying. Your love assures me that my time spent alone with you is never wasted. The illimitable greatness you embody ensures that my time spent praying will be my most treasured experience and most thrilling adventure.

Signed

God, you are my rock and my salvation. All I am is dependent on everything you are. You are my hope for the future, my source for transformation, my helper and my guide. I commit to praying to you because I long to be connected to you each moment of my life.

Signed

A well-balanced prayer life reveals the fullness of God

Approach • Acknowledge

Appreciate • Admit

Ask • Advocate

"...in everything by prayer and supplication with thanksgiving, let your requests be made known to God. And the peace of God which surpasses understanding will guard your hearts and minds in Christ Jesus." Philippians 4:6-7

A prayer for you today

Jesus, we want to experience the fullness of who you are while we are on earth. Teach us to commune with you in a way that activates every facet of your being. Fill our hearts with every quality and attribute you possess. For your glory alone, Amen.

Every relationship requires a certain

My Personal Revelations

112

degree of balance for each person to experience the full vitality of all the relationship offers. Your relationship with God is no different. Your relationship with God must comprise a well-balanced prayer life for you to experience the fullness of who He is, what He does and why He does it. To help you cultivate a well-balanced prayer life, Jesus spoke a prayer (known as the Lord's Prayer) that makes use of six A's:

- Approach
- Acknowledge
- Appreciate
- Admit
- Ask
- Advocate

Using this structure in prayer enables you to engage God in a way that activates the fullness of His identity. On the following page is a list of the six A's and a description of what each 'A' represents.

"...in everything by prayer and supplication with thanksgiving, let your requests be made known to God. And the peace of God which surpasses understanding will guard your hearts and minds in Christ Jesus."
Philippians 4:6-7

Six A's of Prayer

Approach

Humbly • Gratefully • Righteously • Confidently

Acknowledge

Who God Is • Where God Is • What God Does

Appreciate

What God Has Done • What God Is Doing
What God Has Yet To Do

Admit

Admit your sin • Repent of your sin

Ask

Ask God for His eternal regenerative qualities

Ask God to fulfill His every promise

Advocate

Advocate on behalf of other people

<u>Taking Action</u>

Believer, experiencing the totality of God through prayer requires a prayer structure capable of revealing and revering God for everything He is, does and deserves. Applying the six A's of prayer in a well-balanced manner enables you to speak to God with greater intention as it empowers you to bolster the portions of prayer in which you are weak. Each portion of prayer is of equal importance and to experience the wholeness of God, your prayers must embody each portion with equal measure. Today's Taking Action presents a simple exercise that will enable you to understand the meaning and purpose of each portion of prayer. On the following page, the six A's are listed as well as a description of each 'A'. I invite you to take action by matching each description with the 'A' it describes.

Day 8 I Taking Action on following page

<u>Day 8</u>

Taking Action

Match each 'A' to its description by drawing a line to connect them.

After doing so, reflect on the meaning and purpose of each 'A'.

1. Approach

2. Acknowledge

3. Appreciate

4. Admit

5. Ask

6. Advocate

a. Confessing my every thought, word, behavior, action and inaction that causes distance between God and me

b. Thanking God by expressing gratitude for everything that comes my way in this life

c. Presenting myself to God in a manner worthy of bringing Him glory

d. Pleading with God for another person's salvation, spiritual walk and/or temporal needs

e. Exalting God by expressing to Him my awareness of who He is, where He is and what He does

f. Petitioning God for the anointing of His Spirit, the filling of His Spirit and the fulfillment of His promises

Answers: 1c, 2e, 3b, 4a, 5f, 6d

HOW TO PRAY

In Luke 11:1, Jesus' disciples said to Him:

"Lord, teach us to pray."

To which He replied,

"When you pray, pray like this:

Jesus' Model Prayer

Our Father **(Approach)**

[who is] in heaven, hallowed be your name **(Acknowledge)**

Your kingdom come, your will be done, on earth as it is in heaven **(Appr)**

Give us this day our daily bread, **(Ask)**

and forgive us our debts, as we also have forgiven our debtors **(Admit)**

And lead us not into temptation but deliver us from evil **(Ask)**

For yours is the kingdom and the power, and the glory forever

---

The Lord's Prayer is *Jesus' Model Prayer*. In it we see an Approach, an Acknowledgement, an Appreciation, an Admission and an Asking. We also see Jesus advocating for others as He prays using the words: our, we and us.

Jesus' Model Prayer is exactly that — *a model that serves as an example for how we ought to pray.* As we dissect *Jesus' Model Prayer*, we discover how we ought to pray to experience the fullness of God the way Jesus did.

119

<u>Using Jesus' Model Prayer</u>

Our Father in heaven, you alone are sacred and set apart.

Let us as a people exalt you, come to know you and worship your Son

who died for us. Present us blameless and holy in your sight through

the redemptive power of Jesus' life, death and resurrection.

Fulfill your promises to us that you have written in your Holy Word

and provide for every need we have according to your riches in glory

found in Christ. As we confess our sins, be faithful and just, forgiving

and cleansing us from all unrighteousness. Remain faithful and do

not let us be tempted beyond our ability, but when we are tempted,

provide the way of escape so that we may be able to endure it.

In everything, may you receive glory.

It is in your Son's name we pray, Amen.

<u>Taking Action</u>

For today's Taking Action, use *Jesus' Model Prayer* as an example for

how to pray. Absorb Jesus' words into your heart as you allow His

prayer to help you speak to Him a prayer that resembles His.

Our Father
(Approach)

[who is] in heaven,
hallowed be Your name
(Acknowledge)

Your kingdom come, your will be
done on earth as it is in heaven
(Appreciate)

Give us this day our daily bread,
(Ask)

and forgive us our debts, as we
also have forgiven our debtors
(Admit)

And lead us not into temptation
but deliver us from evil
(Ask)

For yours is the kingdom and the
power, and the glory forever

Amen

Amen

10

<u>Prayer as a dialogue</u>

Communicating to God is enabled by prayer, and in one sense, prayer is a dialogue wherein you speak to God using words. As you approach God, acknowledge Him, appreciate Him, admit to Him, ask of Him and advocate for others, you often do so with words. And God, whether He is initiating conversation or responding to your prayer, speaks to you much the same way—through His written Word.

The Bible (God's Word) was written long ago by numerous authors to numerous groups of people. Yet every book of the Bible was written *for you*. It was written for you to see how God relates to His people. It was written for you so you would come to know God and experience who He is. And ultimately, it was written for you to see, feel, and receive the glory of Jesus.

Christian, to truly learn how to pray, you must read the Bible.

To pray effectively you must read and absorb God's Word into your mind until you develop the mind of Christ. That is, until you think, feel, speak, behave and act just as Jesus did and does.

As you commit to absorbing God's Word into your mind, His personal qualities and abilities manifest within you through the supernatural work of the Holy Spirit. Likewise, as you receive God's Word as truth

122

and respond to His Word with faith and obedience, you enable everything God is and does to penetrate your mind and fill your heart until God Himself provokes within you *transformation*.

Believer, take pleasure in knowing that your Bible is the Word of God and differs from every other book you own, whereby every word on every page is alive and breathed out by God. Recognize and acknowledge that God both gains your attention and responds to your prayers through His written Word.

As you venture through each of the six A's of prayer over the next twenty days, you will be presented with a framework designed to empower you to experience the fullness of God. Each day comprises a **How To Overview** (How to approach God, acknowledge God, etc.) and **God's Word with Commentary**.

Each of the six A's also presents you with the opportunity to speak with God face-to-face during a **TALK TO JESUS Prayer Session**.

A *TALK TO JESUS Prayer Session* is your quality time spent alone with God wherein God speaks directly to you and you to Him, by way of the TALK TO JESUS Prayer Session Matrix.

Each Prayer Session Matrix consists of a **Purpose**, a **Universal Prayer**, **God's Word**, a moment of **Reflection and Absorption** on God's Word, *a **Memorization Exercise, Pathway to Your Prayer** and **Your Prayer**.*

Below is a description of each component of the
Prayer Session Matrix followed by a Prayer Session DEMO.
For today's Taking Action, familiarize yourself with each component
of the Prayer Session Matrix and take time to sample the
Prayer Session DEMO on pages 127-128.

Purpose – This is your purpose for praying. The *Purpose* component
of the Prayer Session Matrix serves as your intention for praying or
the subject of the message you intend to convey to God. In this
Prayer Session DEMO, your purpose for praying is to "approach God
with a longing for righteousness and a desire for a powerful prayer
life." View <u>PURPOSE</u> in the Prayer Session DEMO on page 127.

Universal Prayer – This prayer prepares you to hear God's Word. The
Universal Prayer component of the Prayer Session Matrix serves as a
general prayer relevant to your intended purpose for praying. In this
Prayer Session DEMO, the Universal Prayer inspires you to present
yourself to God with an attitude of humility and a spirit of
dependency. View <u>UNIVERSAL PRAYER</u> in the Prayer Session DEMO
on page 127.

God's Word – This is God speaking to you! *God's Word* is a passage
of scripture that relates to your intended purpose for praying. In this

124

Prayer Session DEMO, God says to you "the prayer of a righteous person has great power as it is working" James 5:16b.
View GOD'S WORD in the Prayer Session DEMO on page 127.

Reflect – The *Reflection* component of the Prayer Session Matrix serves as a brief overview of the intended meaning of God's Word *for the people to whom it was directly written.* Reflection calls for you to take a moment to reflect upon why the Word was written, what the author's intent was, how God's Word shaped the world at that time and what effect His Word had on the people to whom it was written. View REFLECT in the Prayer Session DEMO on page 127.

Absorb – The *Absorption* component of the Prayer Session Matrix serves as a brief overview of God's intended message *for you.* Absorption calls for you to think deeply about what God is saying, and to allow what is being said to penetrate your mind until your thoughts, emotions, attitude and actions conform to that of Christ Jesus. View ABSORB in the Prayer Session DEMO on pages 127-128.

Pathway To Your Prayer – The *Pathway To Your Prayer* component of the Prayer Session Matrix serves as a starting point for *Your Prayer* (see following page). *Pathway To Your Prayer* allows you to easily transition from hearing from God through His Word, to then speaking to Him in prayer. View PATHWAY TO YOUR PRAYER in the Prayer Session DEMO on page 128.

Your Prayer – This is your opportunity to speak with God face-to-face! *Your Prayer* is your intimate time spent alone with God in heartfelt dialogue. View YOUR PRAYER in the Prayer Session DEMO on page 128.

Memorization Exercise – The *Memorization Exercise* component of the Prayer Session Matrix is a simple memorization technique wherein you fill in each blank line with specific words used in God's Word. View MEMORIZATION EXERCISE in the Prayer Session DEMO on page 128.

Prayer Session DEMO

PURPOSE | **Approach God**

Approach God with a longing for righteousness

and a desire for a powerful prayer life

UNIVERSAL PRAYER
|

Gracious Lord, I present myself to you with a spirit of dependency and

an attitude of humility. I have been made righteous by you, through

you and for you. In you alone, I put my confidence.

"The prayer of a righteous person has great power as it is working."
|
GOD'S WORD · *James 5:16b*

REFLECT
|

In this passage of scripture, James is encouraging his readers to

present themselves righteous before God so they might activate His

authoritative power through powerful praying.

ABSORB
|

James' message is for you as much as it was for his initially intended

readers. Through the words of James, God is calling on you to

approach Him with a spirit that is completely dependent upon Him.

Through James 5:16, God is saying to you, "If you will honor my Word

by obeying my Word, ask whatever you desire (healing, blessing,

change of circumstance, etc.), and your prayers will cause things to happen for my eternal glory and your eternal good."

"The prayer of a righteous person has great power as it is working."
James 5:16b

Jesus, you readily offer me the gift of prayer, and I long to engage you with it so I can draw closer to you. As I approach you, see to it that I present myself with a heart of humility, an attitude of righteousness and a spirit of confidence.

Hear my prayer as I approach you…

YOUR PRAYER

____

____

____

____

____

____

MEMORIZATION EXERCISE

"The prayer of a _____________________ person has great ___________ as it is working." James 5:16b

APPROACH GOD

Fasting Introduced

Christian fasting is for anyone who is passionate about pursuing Jesus. Fasting is not a means of manipulating God for something you want, nor is it a legalistic duty demanded by God. Rather, fasting is fulfilling your desire to pursue Jesus more passionately by sacrificing a God-given passion and replacing that passion with your craving for Christ. Choosing to fast will enable you to experience deeper intimacy with God throughout this 40 Day Journey and thereafter.

Fasting is optional; however, be encouraged to challenge yourself to take a break from something you regularly enjoy and replace that time with your passion to know and experience Jesus.

Ask yourself:

What am I passionate about?

What good gift from God do I regularly enjoy?

Are you passionate about food? Are you passionate about spending quality time with your family and friends? Are you passionate about specific hobbies and/or activities?

Three times during this journey you will be encouraged to list a God-given passion you are willing to take a break from so that you can more passionately pursue Christ through His Word, prayer and/or love in action.

Approach God with Humility

Approach
Humbly • Gratefully
Righteously • Confidently

A prayer for you today

Jesus, you gave life to God's promises when you died for our sins, and you put your power on display when you rose from the grave. As we acknowledge your power and glory, we are humbled. We are humbled to receive your mercy and grace, and we are humbled to be made fully alive to God through you. With humility in our mind and surrender in our hearts, we approach you, Amen.

Humility arises as you acknowledge and embrace your need for and your dependency on God, and it is with this thought in mind that today's *How To*

Humility arises as you acknowledge and embrace your need for and your dependency on God

---

My Personal Revelations

____

____

____

____

____

____

____

____

____

____

____

____

131

Overview is written.

Rather than writing from the perspective you have been accustomed to reading, Day 11 is written from *your perspective*, as if you have written the words yourself.

As you read today's *How To Overview,* be encouraged speak to yourself the importance of humility, and acknowledging and embracing your need for and your dependency on your heavenly Father.

Speak these words to yourself –

"I would not exist if God did not create me. I would not be able to accomplish anything had God not provided me the talent, skill and ability. And most imperatively, I would be spending my eternity separated from God forever had He not chosen to redeem me through the life, death and resurrection of His Son, Christ. I am alive only because God wills that I live. I think, walk, talk and do *solely because of God.*

"The reward for humility and fear of the LORD is riches and honor and life."
Proverbs 22:4

132

In my fight to embrace humility, I must

begin by acknowledging the fact that I

am nothing more than a human being

created by God from the ground I walk

on. I am not the center of the universe

and people were not put here to worship

me. Nor was I put here to worship

myself. Daily I must choose to embody a

healthy fear of God as I commit to

developing a reverence for His love, His

power and His qualities and abilities.

Today I choose to live my life not as if I

created myself or as if my plans are

better than God's plan; rather I am

choosing to take my eyes off myself so I

can gaze at the glory of Jesus' life, death

and resurrection, and humbly embrace

all that Jesus is for me."

Claim these words by signing your name.

(God's Word with commentary)

"Jesus, who though he was in the form of God, did not count equality with God a thing to be grasped, but emptied himself, by taking the form of a servant, being born in the likeness of men. And being found in human form, he humbled himself by becoming obedient to the point of death, even death on a cross." Philippians 2:6-8

Jesus approached the world with humility. He allowed Himself to be placed in our hands to the point of death, trusting His Father had a plan. My friend, determine to approach God the same way Jesus approached the world. Approach God with humility by placing your life in His hands and trusting that His plan for you is far greater than the plans you have for yourself.

"But he gives more grace. Therefore it says, 'God opposes the proud but gives grace to the humble'." James 4:6

If you choose to approach God having an attitude of pride, you will limit the blessings God desires to give you.

"The reward for humility and fear of the LORD is riches and honor and life."
Proverbs 22:4

When you fear the Lord, you will likewise be humbled. To fear God means to live in awe of His power and to reject everything that is evil. The reward for living such a way assures you of the blessings that come through knowing and emulating Jesus.

"Humble yourselves, therefore, under the mighty hand of God so that at the proper time he may exalt you."
1 Peter 5:6

If you live humbly, you will be exalted— perhaps in this life or the next. It is God who determines the proper time you are to be exalted. Therefore, trust His good

timing as you strive to live out each
moment of your life with a humble
attitude and a humble state of mind.

<u>Taking Action</u>

God created you to perfection and He
did so without any input from you. Daily,
God chooses to enrich you with talents,
gifts and abilities, and His sole purpose
for doing so is to empower you to carry
out His will and reveal His glory.

To be humble, you must embrace the
fact that every talent, gift and ability you
possess comes from above and is in no
way created or fully sustained by you.
Put another way, to be humble, you
must live with a steady conscious
awareness of God's provision as you
acknowledge moment by moment your
dependency on all He provides. God
alone is the Creator and Sustainer and
you are only able to develop and sustain
your God-given talents, gifts and abilities
because God gives you the ability to do
so and wills that you do so.

136

Nevertheless, rejoice knowing that **your ability is God's glory**, and He graciously invites you to partake in His glory by enacting His works and carrying out His will.

For today's Taking Action, acknowledge and reflect upon the multitude of talents, gifts and abilities with which God has blessed you. In doing so, take action by listing one talent, one gift and one ability that you consider impactful to who you are and who you are becoming. Upon completing your list, reflect on how your life might be different had God not created you with, and progressively sustained for you the talent, gift and ability you listed. Allow this reflection to remind you of your need for God and your dependency upon all He provides.

Day 11 I Taking Action on following page

"But he gives more grace. Therefore it says, 'God opposes the proud but gives grace to the humble'." James 4:6

<u>Day 11</u>

Taking Action

Ponder the multitude of talents, gifts and abilities God has entrusted to you. In doing so, list one talent, one gift and one ability that you believe impacts who you are and who you are becoming. Example responses are included below.

Talent:

____

I am a talented writer

Gift:

____

I have the gift of kindness

Ability:

____

I have the ability to lead

As you view your list, recognize that your talent, gift and ability is given to you and sustained for you by God and His provision. Be humbled knowing *God's greatness* is the reason your talents, gifts and abilities exist.

12

Approach God Gratefully

Approach
Humbly • **Gratefully**
Righteously • Confidently

A prayer for you today

Jesus, birth in us a grateful regard for everything that comes our way in this life. See to it that your eternal blessings become the source of our grateful disposition as you free us from our attitude of self-righteousness and self-entitlement. We pray in your great name, Amen.

How often do you pause your daily activities simply to awe at the beauty of all God has created for you to enjoy? God created this world for you so you might approach life gratefully and experience life as a joyful adventure.

To follow God's will you must approach Him with a grateful heart

---

My Personal Revelations

139

God has provided for you everything you need to live your life with inner peace and unrelenting joy. You have breath; you have life; and through God's mercy and grace, you have been gifted with a faith that breaks the chains of your enslavement to sin, whereby enabling you to live your life in ultimate freedom. Believer, allow the reality of these truths to produce within you a grateful regard for God, for people and for life! Refuse to walk through life as if God owes you something or as if the world revolves around you. Be thankful for a God who provides! Likewise, respect the good in other people by taking an interest in them and acknowledging their self-worth. Surely, self-righteousness and self-entitlement feeds the ungrateful heart. Having an attitude of "I did this!" and "I deserve that!" works against God's plan for your life, not for it.

To truly follow God's will, you must acknowledge your dependency on God and His provision. To truly follow God's

"...give thanks in all circumstances; for this is the will of God in Christ Jesus for you."
1 Thessalonians 5:18

140

will, you must approach Him with a
grateful heart.

"...give thanks in all circumstances; for this is the will of God in Christ Jesus for you." 1 Thessalonians 5:18

Approach God with a grateful disposition by giving Him thanks for everything. Thanksgiving ought to be inseparably joined with prayer as you seek God's will for your life.

"Do not be anxious about anything, but in everything by prayer and supplication with thanksgiving let your requests be made known to God." Philippians 4:6

Recognize that every moment of prayer must be enriched with thankfulness toward God lest it not be accepted.

"Enter his gates with thanksgiving, and his courts with praise! Give thanks to him; bless his name!"
Psalm 100:4

Enter God's presence with a profound
sense of gratitude and thanksgiving.
It is with this heart that you give Him
praise and bless His name.

Taking Action

Approaching God with a grateful heart
brings glory to God as it expresses to Him
your satisfaction in all He does. As a
reward to you, approaching life with a
grateful disposition produces within you
feelings of joy, satisfaction and peace.
For today's Taking Action, express your
gratitude to God in writing by telling Him
why you are grateful for the talent, gift
and ability you listed on Day 11. Think
deeply about what each of these
blessings means to you and why you
appreciate God for them as you talk to
Jesus.

142

<u>Day 12</u>

Taking Action

Reflect on the talent, gift and ability you listed on Day 11, and express

to God why you are grateful to enjoy each blessing.

As you speak to Him in prayer, examine the depth of

your humility by asking yourself:

Am I glorying God with each blessing, or

am I glorifying myself?

Talent: ______________________

Gift: ______________________

Ability: ______________________

13

Approach God Righteously

Approach
Humbly • Gratefully
Righteously • Confidently

A prayer for you today

Jesus, you know our every thought, every spoken word and every action and inaction. See to it that we live our lives with righteous intent. Liken our attitude and actions to yours as you transform our hearts by renewing our minds.
We pray in your name, Amen.

You are more at peace with yourself and God when you live your life honorably. When you overcome temptations by responding to situations and circumstances in a God-fearing way, you open yourself up to being filled with righteousness.   Recognize that as you

You are more at peace with yourself and God when you live your life honorably

---

My Personal Revelations

____

____

____

____

____

____

____

____

____

____

____

____

144

practice righteousness, you are made righteous (1 John 2:29). Only by living in a righteous manner can you be certain you are on the right path and following the will of God.

Examine yourself. Assess your thoughts, your speech, your attitude and your actions.

Are you practicing righteousness? Believer, approach God with the freedom of a clean conscience. Approach Him without guilt in your heart or tension in your mind as you fight daily to obey His commands and uphold His Word. In doing so, your conversations with Him will feel more alive, and your prayers will bestow more power.

"Little children, let no one deceive you. Whoever practices righteousness is righteous, as he is righteous."
1 John 3:7

Having been saved by grace through faith, you are being anointed and filled with the Spirit of God daily. It is both your privilege and your responsibility to be controlled by the Holy Spirit and to practice His righteousness.

"He who walks righteously...he will dwell on the heights; his place of defense will be the fortresses of rocks; his bread will be given him; his water will be sure. Your eyes will behold the king in his beauty; they will see a land that stretches afar."
Isaiah 33:15-17

As you walk righteously, you are sure to experience face-to-face fellowship with your Father. God will be your protection and your source for a prosperous life. He will supply your body and soul's every need.

"The prayer of a righteous person has great power as it is working."
James 5:16b

As you allow the Holy Spirit to declare you righteous, your prayers become a dynamic force capable of activating God's power to do the unimaginable.

Taking Action

Practicing righteousness manifests itself in four ways: thinking righteously, speaking righteously, behaving righteously and acting righteously.

Thought – Do you find yourself thinking negatively about yourself or someone else?

Think righteously by changing your mind.

Speech – Do you speak negatively to yourself? Do you speak harshly to others or God?

Practice righteousness by speaking only that which builds yourself and others up.

Attitude – What is your attitude at work, school and home? Are you representing Christ well?

Have the attitude of righteousness by refusing to boast, complain, grumble or mope.

147

Act – Are you willfully opposing God by acting in a way that dishonors Him? Are you refusing to do things you know God is calling you to do?

Act righteously by embracing self-control and overcoming temptation. Likewise, act righteously by showing your faith through good works.

For today's Taking Action, practice righteousness by thinking righteously. Your speech, attitude and actions are often a product of the way you think, therefore the discipline of thinking righteously serves as the catalyst for practicing every other form of righteousness.

How and what you think affects you. That is, your thoughts often influence the way you feel, and your feelings often influence the way you speak, behave and act. All things considered, your thoughts are the ignition switch that activates all you are, say and do.

Reflect for a moment on the difference between how you feel when your thoughts are peaceful versus how you feel when your thoughts are negative. When you are thinking pleasant thoughts, naturally you feel at peace. However, when your thoughts are exceedingly negative, you tend to feel just as downcast as your destructive thought pattern.

Dr. Martin Lloyd Jones, a British preacher, author and medical doctor, addressed negative thinking patterns and how to defeat them in a quote from his book, "Spiritual Depression: It's Causes and Cures". In it he writes, "Have you realized that most of your unhappiness in life is due to the fact that you are listening to yourself instead of talking to yourself? Take those thoughts that come to you the moment you wake up in the morning. You have not originated them but they are talking to you, they bring back the problems of yesterday, etc. Somebody is talking. Who is talking to you? Your self

"The prayer of a righteous person has great power as it is working."
James 5:16b

is talking to you." He goes on to reference King David's negative self-talk and how he overcame it in Psalm 42. "Now this man's treatment [King David] was this: instead of allowing this [negative] self to talk to him, he starts talking to himself. 'Why art thou downcast, O my soul?' he asks. His soul had been depressing him, crushing him. So he stands up and says, 'Self, listen for a moment, I will speak to you!'"

Believer, what this means is you must control the way you think by speaking into your mind the truths found in scripture. If God tells you "you can do all things through Christ who strengthens you" (Philippians 4:13), why do you tell yourself you cannot? If God tells you He has "given you a spirit of power, love and self-control" (2 Timothy 1:7), why do you act as if you have no power, as if you cannot forgive and as if you cannot control the way you think?

The Bible says, **"whatever is true, whatever is honorable, whatever is just,**

whatever is pure, whatever is lovely,
whatever is commendable, if there is
any excellence, if there is anything
worthy of praise, think about these
things" Philippians 4:8.**

From this day forward, determine to
speak the truth about yourself, *to
yourself!*

- "If God is for me, who can be
  against me?" (Romans 8:31)
- "I can do all things through Christ
  who strengthens me."
  (Philippians 4:13)
- "All things will work together for
  my good." (Romans 8:28)

Determine to feed on the truths found in
scripture until the thoughts you have
about yourself, others and God comes
solely from the mind and mouth of God!
In doing so, your feelings about yourself
will change, and consequently so will your
speech, attitude and actions.

**The battle to practice righteousness
begins in your mind, and I encourage you
from this day forward to practice
righteousness by thinking righteously.**

151

Taking Action

Take control of your mind by thinking righteously. Recognize and identify two negative thoughts that weaken you and/or tear others down. Thereafter, replace these negative thoughts with thoughts of truth—*thoughts worthy of building yourself and others up.* Once you replace your negative thoughts with truths found in scripture, absorb God's Word into your mind until it does its job of transforming the way you think about yourself, others and God. Explore your Bible and/or this book for scriptures to use as truth replacements.

Below is an example of a negative thought
and a truth replacement.

Negative thought

"I cannot do anything right or accomplish any of the desires I set out to accomplish."

Truth replacement

"I can do all things through Christ who strengthens me."
"Jesus provides for me the ability to succeed. He knows my heart's desires, and He is working with me to see that His will for my life comes to pass. I am determined to do all things through Christ who strengthens me."

Negative thought:

Truth replacement:

Negative thought:

Truth replacement:

14

Approach God with Confidence

Approach
Humbly • Gratefully
Righteously • **Confidently**

A prayer for you today

Jesus, separate us from our fears, doubts
and uncertainties, and flood
our hearts with a confidence that
remembers, believes and trusts.
Reveal yourself to us through your Word
and manifest within us as we absorb
your truths and respond to them.
We trust you, and in you we have great
confidence. Blessed be your name,
Amen.

Remember

Recall who you were before God saved
you. Reflect on the quality of character
of your old self and compare that person

**God has the power to
change you as well as any
situation or circumstance
you are in**

My Personal Revelations

to the person you are today. It is through this remembrance that you experience the confidence of knowing that with God, all things are possible. God has the power to change you as well as any situation or circumstance you are in. God has the power to transform anyone into a new person.

You are proof of that.

Believe

To believe is to receive Jesus as your source for truth, power and wisdom so that He takes away your desire to search for these virtues anywhere outside of Him. Believing is the assured hope that Jesus is able, faithful and willing to meet your needs and satisfy your soul's hunger so that your quest for satisfaction remains in Him. This *believing and being satisfied* does not happen by consuming all the temporary pleasures of the world and then coming to Christ out of obligation or duty. Your satisfaction in Christ—and the

"Until now you have asked nothing in my name. Ask, and you will receive, that your joy may be full." John 16:24

confidence that follows—arises as you create intimacy with Him through prayer and respond obediently to His Word.

Trust

Trust God by trusting His Word and the insights His Word provokes. The world, in all its sin, is filled with deception and readily offers you a false sense of reality. Therefore, to fulfill your destiny and become the truest sense of who you are in Christ, you must read and heed the Word of God. **You must trust God by trusting His Word rather than trusting the world's wisdom**. Only then can you approach God with confidence knowing He is able, faithful and willing to fulfill every promise He has made to you.

"Beloved, if our heart does not condemn us, we have confidence before God; and whatever we ask we receive from him, because we keep his commandments and do what pleases him." 1 John 3:21

156

As you live in accordance with the Word of God and desire His will above your own, you can ask God for anything, and receive from Him just as you ask.

And Jesus answered them, "Have faith in God. Truly, I say to you, whoever says to this mountain, 'Be taken up and thrown into the sea,' and does not doubt in his heart, but believes that what he says will come to pass, it will be done for him. Therefore I tell you, whatever you ask in prayer, believe that you have received it, and it will be yours." Mark 11:22-24

Strive to develop a confidence in God that believes He can accomplish what seems impossible to you, with infinite ease.

"Until now you have asked nothing in my name. Ask, and you will receive, that your joy may be full." John 16:24

It should give you great confidence knowing Jesus wants to give you what you ask for. He wants to reward you and bless you so that your joy remains full.

Taking Action

You are more than one third of the way through 40 days and you have accomplished much. You have committed to developing a healthy, well-balanced relationship with God through prayer. You have prayed as Jesus prayed. You were introduced to the Prayer Session Matrix. And in the past three days you have embraced humility, expressed gratitude and practiced righteousness!

Be confident knowing God is responding to your prayers as you commit to spending at least ten minutes of quality time per day with Him. Through your prayers, God is enriching a spiritual attribute in your life, and He is working things for His glory and for the good of the person for whom you have been praying.

For today's Taking Action, join with others in praying the prayer below. Together, we will acknowledge God as trustworthy and express to Him our confidence in His ability and willingness to fulfill His promises and accomplish our heart's desires. After praying, take a moment to speak to God alone, acknowledging Him for every revelation and measure of growth you have experienced thus far in your TALK TO JESUS journey.

Day 14 I Taking Action on following page

159

<u>Day 14</u>

Taking Action

A prayer of for you

Father, together with fellow believers who have gone and will go through this 40 Day Journey, we acknowledge you as trustworthy, and we receive your Word as truth. We are confident in your ability and have faith in your willingness to fulfill every promise you have made to us. Continue to draw close to us as we call on you through prayer and meditate on the scriptures and insights written in this book. We love and adore you, God. It is in your Son's name we pray. Amen.

Speak to God for a moment as you reflect upon the past
two weeks of daily readings and action invitations.
Acknowledge God for every revelation and measure of growth you
have experienced thus far in your TALK TO JESUS journey.
Feel free to use the writing space below.

160

15

Approach God

Approach God as a child in the arms of a loving Father

My Father, you are in control, and you know what is best for me. I look to you alone for truth, love and wisdom and as the One who provides my every need. I am who I am because of who you are—my Creator and my loving Father—and I approach you with humility, gratitude and confidence and a desire to do what honors you and brings you glory.

"But now, O LORD, you are our Father; we are the clay, and you are our potter; we are all the work of your hand." Isaiah 64:8

REFLECT

In this passage of scripture, the prophet Isaiah is speaking to God on behalf of the nation of Israel—acknowledging God as "Father" and God's people as the Father's clay. In this portion of Isaiah's prayer, Isaiah is giving God full authority and reign over the nation of Israel

and pleading with God to mold and shape them into the people
He wants them to be.

ABSORB

Believer, God has more love and compassion to give to you than any amount of love and compassion you will receive from another person. Whether your earthly father has been good to you, bad to you, non-existent or anything in between, I encourage you to strive to see your *heavenly Father* for who He truly is and to approach Him with the awe, reverence and honor He deserves. Your heavenly Father is all-knowing, all-loving, all-good and all-satisfying, and everything you receive from Him in this life and the life to come is for your good. Therefore, approach God—*your never-failing, always faithful eternal Father*—with the utmost humility, gratitude, confidence and respect.

"But now, O LORD, you are our Father; we are the clay, and you are our potter; we are all the work of your hand." Isaiah 64:8

Father, I trust you. I place my life in your loving hands and put my full weight on you. I believe that whatever I receive in this life—however pleasing or displeasing it seems—is for my good because you are good. Therefore, in every experience and in every happening, I will look to you as my Father, and humbly embrace all that you are to me through the life, death and resurrection of your Son, Jesus.

Hear my prayer as I approach you with childlike trust and childlike faith...

"But now, O LORD, you are our ______________; we are the clay, and you are our potter; we are all the _________ of your _________."

Isaiah 64:8

ACKNOWLEDGE GOD

Fast

List a God-given passion you regularly enjoy and plan a specific time to fast from this passion on one occasion over the next three days. **During your time of fasting, have a purpose for your fast.**

Your purpose for fasting can range from:

- Focusing your mind solely on God's Word and the insights His Word provokes
- Speaking God's truths back to Him through prayer
- Praying for yourself or someone else
- Sharing the love of Jesus with another person through love in action (act of love/service carried out in Jesus' name)

Your God-Given Passion (e.g. Eating):

____

Specified Time of Fasting (e.g. Dinnertime on Day 17):

____

Your Purpose For Fasting:

____

____

____

16

Acknowledge God for who He is

Acknowledge
Who He Is • Where He Is
What He Does

God is infinite and timeless; He has always been and will never cease to be

A prayer for you

Jesus, you revealed God to the world by living your life in perfect harmony with the Father. You demonstrated for us the qualities and character of God, and in doing so, you became His perfect image. As we acknowledge God for who He is, let us look no further than who you were as a man, and who you are as the eternal Son of God. Amen.

My Personal Revelations

God never had a beginning. He is infinite and timeless; He has always been and will never cease to be.

God is everywhere. He is the reality of everything seen and unseen. He is not

167

dependent on anything or anyone; He does as He pleases and has no limits or constraints.

God is absolutely Holy. God cannot and does not change. He is absolutely perfect and His absolute perfection cannot be made better.

God is the essence of love. There is no love without God, and there is no love outside of God, because God is love.

God is the Spiritual Father to every person who is born-again. God takes residence in the heart of every believer and becomes the believer's hope, the believer's Savior and Lord of the believer's life.

God has made Himself known. God revealed Himself to all men by becoming a man Himself. Jesus Christ is the visible image of the invisible God. **"He is the radiance of God's glory and the exact imprint of [God's] nature"** (Hebrews 1:3a).

Believer, above all, God is a person who desires to know you and be known by you. As you acknowledge God for who He is, consider your pursuit of knowing Him greater than every other venture you pursue.

"I am the Alpha and the Omega, the first and the last, the beginning and the end." Revelation 22:13

Your heavenly Father originated the plan for salvation, and He will bring it to completion. No one came before God and no one will come after Him. In the end, everyone will confess that Jesus is Lord.

"[There is] one God and Father of all, who is over all and through all and in all." Ephesians 4:6

God is the one and only God, the Father to all men and the Spiritual Father to all who believe. God works

through those who acknowledge Him for
who He truly is, and He carries out His
plan for the world by the power of His
Holy Spirit.

___

"Anyone who does not love does not
know God, because God is love."
1 John 4:8

___

God is the essence of love and His love is
infinitely worthy. He is the continuous
stream of mercy and grace that is
poured out for you daily through the life,
death and resurrection of His Son.

___

"You who are of purer eyes than to see
evil and cannot look at wrong."
Habakkuk 1:13a

___

God is absolutely holy, and in the
presence of His absolute holiness, sin
cannot and does not exist.

"[There is] one God and
Father of all, who is over
all and through all and in
all." Ephesians 4:6

170

Acknowledging someone expresses to that person your awareness of who they are. When you acknowledge God for who He truly is, you honor Him by esteeming Him for His personal qualities and abilities. For today's Taking Action, acknowledge God by naming Him. Make use of the full alphabet (A-Z) to comprise names for God wherein each name you give God begins with a specific letter of the alphabet.

Take your time and have fun with it! If you cannot come up with a name for a letter, don't fret. If you think of two or three names for a letter, feel free to write them in! This is your time to acknowledge God by naming and exalting Him for who He truly is.

Day 16 I Taking Action on following page

<u>Day 16</u>

Taking Action

Acknowledge God for **who He is** by naming Him using the alphabet.

A	N
B	O
C	P
D	Q
E	R
F	S
G	T
H	U
I	V
J	W
K	X
L	Y
M	Z

172

17

Acknowledge God for where He is

Acknowledge
Who He Is • **Where He Is**
What He Does

God is always current and can be enjoyed in every present moment

---

A prayer for you

Jesus, we are grateful you have not left us alone. You exist everywhere, even in our hearts. You have chosen to align our spirit with yours, and moment by moment, you are availing yourself to the details of our lives. Hear our hearts as we acknowledge you for where you are. We pray in your name, Amen.

There is no place where God is not present. There is no atom too small and no galaxy too broad for God's existence. God exists everywhere and is present to everything. God cannot be confined by space.

My Personal Revelations

173

God cannot be outrun and cannot be slowed down. God is always current, and He is present in every *now.* He has overseen every historical event and will govern every future happening. God is not limited by time.

God has made His home in heaven where He prepares a room for every person who believes and abides in His Son. In heaven, God is exalted, Jesus is worshiped and peace is made permanent. There is no death, no pain and no tears—only joy.

God has made His home inside you. Though you are a mere body on the outside, you are soul and spirit on the inside. Your spirit is the deepest part of who you are, and your spirit is designed to receive and communicate with the Spirit of God. The moment you received Jesus as Savior and Lord, you received the Spirit of Christ who lives within you.

Christian, acknowledge God as being present in every situation and

174

circumstance; nothing can remove you from the presence of God. Likewise, acknowledge God's home in heaven as the eternal Paradise where God is exalted, Jesus is worshiped and love reigns forever. And with a joyful heart, acknowledge God as being alive inside you, enabling you to hear His voice, speak to Him and carry out His will of producing heaven on earth.

"Be not rash with your mouth, nor let your hearts be hasty to utter a word before God, for God is in heaven and you are on earth. Therefore let your words be few." Ecclesiastes 5:2

Recognize God as sacred and set apart.
He is the Creator of the heavens where
He is worshiped without end.
He is your Final Judge and your source
for never-ending bliss. Acknowledge God
as such, and seek to follow His will rather
than your own.

"Can a man hide himself in secret places so that I cannot see him, declares the LORD. Do I not fill heaven and earth, declares the LORD." Jeremiah 23:24

God is with you wherever you go; there is no place God is not present. In every situation and circumstance, God is working things for His eternal glory and your eternal good. Therefore, acknowledge Him as being omnipresent and let His omnipresence assure you that you are never alone.

"I have been crucified with Christ. It is no longer I who live, but Christ who lives in me." Galatians 2:20

Jesus lives inside every person who has received Him as Lord. As a believer, you are dead to sin and alive to the eternal glory made available through Christ's resurrection. Just as Jesus defeated death, so too have you, through Him.

176

<u>Day 17</u>

Taking action

Acknowledge **where God is** through this James L. Black hymn

<u>God is here, and that to bless us</u>

God is here, and that to bless us
With the Spirit's quick'ning power;
See, the cloud already bending,
Waits to drop the grateful shower.

Let it come, O Lord, we pray Thee,
Let the shower of blessing fall;
We are waiting, we are waiting,
Oh, revive the hearts of all.

God is here! we feel His presence
In this consecrated place;
But we need the soul refreshing
Of His free, unbounded grace.

God is here! oh, then, believing,
Bring to Him our one desire,
That His love may now be kindled,
Till its flame each heart inspire.

Savior, grant the prayer we offer,
While in simple faith we bow,
From the windows of Thy mercy
Pour us out a blessing now.

18

Acknowledge God for what He does

Acknowledge
Who He Is • Where He Is
What He Does

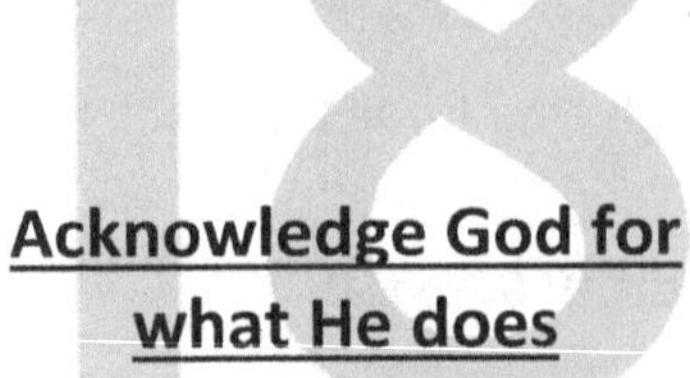

God is the reason for the existence of every good thing

A prayer for you

Jesus, you are the Creator and Designer of all there is. Nothing came before you and nothing exists without you. We acknowledge you today as the source of our provision, and we treasure you for all you do. We pray in your name, Amen.

God is the Creator. He created life and designed the complexities that breed the abilities of every living thing. He continually creates for you the opportunity both to live and to do according to His foreseen plan.

My Personal Revelations

178

God is a definer. He determines the veracity of truth and defines the ingenuity of wisdom. He is the definition of love and the outpouring source of it. God's love is the reason you exist.

God is a good Father. He pours His Spirit into every person who believes and fulfills every promise He has made to those who love Him. Because of His goodness, God became a man and lived among us so we might know and emulate Him. For you and me, God laid down His life.

Christian, God is the reason for the existence of every good thing. In all His power, He created you, He provides for you, and He chose to give you *new life*. Because of God's love, you are redeemed from your transgressions and united again with your Father in heaven. Be forever in awe knowing that the God whom you call "Father" is the Creator of the world, the Ruler and Sustainer of the universe and the only One capable of

"The heart of a man plans his way, but the LORD establishes his steps."
Proverbs 16:9

179

doing what you cannot even imagine!

"Have you not known? Have you not heard? The LORD is the everlasting God, the Creator of the ends of the earth." Isaiah 40:28a

God is everlasting. No one created God; God alone is the Creator. Though we are creators ourselves (having been made in the image of God), we cannot *truly* create. Because in order to create, we must make use of things already created. Every creative gene and every creation of man finds its origin in God.

"The heart of a man plans his way, but the LORD establishes his steps."
Proverbs 16:9

We cannot live outside the parameters that God created for us to live. If we do, we are not truly living. God determined the way, the truth and the life, and He alone paved the way to which it can be found.

"...yet for us there is one God, the Father, from whom are all things and for whom we exist, and one Lord, Jesus Christ, through whom are all things and through whom we exist."
1 Corinthians 8:6

You can acknowledge God as a good Father because He created you with His love, redeemed you by His love and called you to be loved.

Increase your time in prayer → In addition to praying for a filling of one of God's own attributes and for the good of another person, begin acknowledging God for who He is, where He is and all He does during your quality time of prayer. Consider increasing your prayer time to twenty minutes.

Day 18 I Taking Action on following page

181

<u>Day 18</u>

Taking Action

A prayer for you

God, you uphold the world by the power of your Word and work

through your sons and daughters by the power of your Spirit.

Show us your works, Lord. Reveal to us all you are doing through

your children so that your glory is revealed for all to see.

In Jesus' name, Amen.

Are you expressing your faith through good works? Is God working

through you to impact the world and bring about good things? If so,

let others know! Consider the amazing things God is doing through

you by way of your church, your schooling, your career, your family

life and/or your hobbies and activities.

In doing so, post a message, photo or video on TikTok, Instagram and

Facebook using the hashtag #talktojesusbook telling others how God

is working through you to showcase His glory!

Thank you for revealing God's glory for all to see!

Acknowledge God

Acknowledge God as the Creator of all things and as the One to whom glory is owed

Father in heaven, you alone are sacred and set apart.

You are the Creator of all things and you sustain all you created.

You are all-knowing and all-powerful. You are the essence of love,

and you chose to reside in me.

"For by him all things were created, in heaven and on earth, visible and invisible, whether thrones or dominions or rulers or authorities—all things were created through him and for him."

Colossians 1:16

REFLECT

In writing to the church of Colossae, Paul illustrates for them the supremacy, sufficiency and divinity of Christ. In this passage of scripture, Paul is telling his readers that Jesus, in his human nature, is the visible discovery of the invisible God.

183

ABSORB

Outside of Jesus nothing was made that has been made. He is the Creator and Sustainer of all things. Everything in creation, in heaven and on earth, was made by Him, through Him and for His glory.

He is coequal, consubstantial and coeternal with the Father. Jesus is your Creator and your Everlasting Father, and He is worthy of your highest praise and acknowledgement.

"For by him all things were created, in heaven and on earth, visible and invisible, whether thrones or dominions or rulers or authorities—all things were created through him and for him."

Colossians 1:16

Jesus, everything in existence belongs to you and every good thing speaks of your glory. You alone have the power, and therefore you alone shall be glorified.

Hear my prayer as I acknowledge you...

184

"For by him all things were _______________, in heaven and on earth, visible and _______________, whether thrones or dominions or rulers or authorities—all things were created _______________ him and _______ him." Colossians 1:16

APPRECIATE GOD

Fast

List a God-given passion you regularly enjoy and plan a specific time to fast from this passion on one occasion over the next three days. **During your time of fasting, have a purpose for your fast. Fasting is not merely an act of self-deprivation; rather fasting provides for you an opportunity to grow in likeness to Jesus.**

Your God-Given Passion (e.g. Family time):

____

Specified Time of Fasting (e.g. Date night 6pm-8pm on Day 21):

____

Your Purpose For Fasting:

(see page 166 for a list of examples)

____

____

____

____

Appreciate God for what He has done

Appreciate
What He Has Done • What He Is Doing
What He Has Yet To Do

A prayer for you today

Jesus, you have gifted us with eternal

salvation and saved us from eternal

punishment. See to it that the reality of

your life, death and resurrection is

forever on our conscience.

Create within us a desire to express

to you our continual gratitude for your

sacrifice, your loyalty and your gift of

eternal life. Amen.

You fully appreciate God by submitting

to a constant state of dependence on

Him. Having a dependency on and an

appreciation of God is born through a

**You fully appreciate God
by submitting to a constant
state of dependence
on Him**

My Personal Revelations

____

____

____

____

____

____

____

____

____

____

____

steadfast conscious awareness of having been saved by grace through faith. Solely when you live in the reality of knowing that the only thing standing between you and a Godless eternity is *God Himself,* will you be able to fully appreciate God.

Be encouraged to develop a deep appreciation for God by first celebrating God as *Giver.* Daily, God determines to give you grace, faith, hope and provision—*His sun never fails to rise for you, and His Son did not fail to die for you!* Every blessing you receive originates from God and is given to you so you might experience the love that God *is* and become fully satisfied in Him. Furthermore, realize that everything you receive in this life (good or bad) intentionally provides for you an opportunity to grow in likeness to Jesus. In doing so, you will enable yourself to appreciate absolutely everything, because in the path of obedience, everything that happens to you is

"For by grace you have been saved through faith. And this is not of your own doing; it is the gift of God."

Ephesians 2:8

190

conforming you to the likeness of Christ; and great is your reward in heaven when you present yourself to God having been transformed into the image of His Son.

Christian, as you acknowledge God as *Giver* and appreciate the Giver's gifts, allow His gift of salvation to be the one you treasure most. The heaviness of the guilt and shame that was lifted from you when God saved you from His judgment ought to be your source for experiencing unending joy and expressing unending gratitude. Be encouraged to live gratefully by reminding yourself daily of the new life you have been given and of the source from whom it was received.

"Every good gift and every perfect gift is from above, coming down from the Father of lights, with whom there is no variation or shadow due to change."
James 1:17

God gives good gifts and every good gift God gives is perfect. For whatever you receive from God, be thankful. Likewise, for whatever you do not receive from God, *be thankful*—knowing God has a plan and trusting that He is working things for His eternal glory and your eternal good.

"For by grace you have been saved through faith. And this is not of your own doing; it is the gift of God."
Ephesians 2:8

God has given you the gift of faith and through this gift He considers you holy and blameless. Present yourself eternally grateful for having received God's gift of faith, and in everything, give thanks. Let this be the default state of your mind as you remind yourself daily that you were once lost but now you are found.

Taking Action

Without the grace of God, eternal salvation does not exist, and hell is all that remains. Hell is a subject many pastors do not address, although they should. Hell makes people feel uncomfortable, and therefore many people, Christians included, seldom acknowledge its existence.

Though hell scares us (and rightfully so), it does not have to be a subject we avoid. To address hell is simply to address God and His relation to sin— *God is eternally righteous and therefore sin requires an eternally righteous judgement.*

Put another way, *sin separates us from an eternally holy and just God, and therefore sin is the cause for eternal separation.*

Eternity in hell is the reality for everyone living outside of redemption offered through Jesus Christ. Hell is the eternal conscious punishment of those who do not repent and trust in Christ, and as it is described in the Bible: **Hell is an unquenchable fire void of love, joy and peace of any kind. In hell, those who do**

**not repent and trust in Christ "will
suffer the punishment of eternal
destruction, away from the presence of
the Lord and the glory of his might"
2 Thessalonians 1:9.**

*Pause for a moment to reflect on the
unfortunate reality of hell. As you do,
imagine for a moment the type of place
hell really is until it unsettles you.*

As you ponder the harsh reality of hell, it
is important for you to realize that hell,
as described above, *was your reality* had
it not been for the free gift of grace you
received from God.
Can you feel the weight of that?
Jesus saved you from a never-ending
suffering! He saved you from an eternal
torment that persists day after day, year
after year, decade after decade and
millennium after millennium. And He did
so on His own *with no help from you!*
Your acknowledgment of this intense
reality ought to fill you with the deepest

194

appreciation for God, who in His mercy, poured His grace over you and said, "You are forgiven! Come and rest in Me."

For today's Taking Action, prayer with fellow believers who have and are reading this book. Together, we will appreciate God for saving us from His judgment, from a life of eternal punishment and from an earthly life void of Him. After praying, take a moment to speak to God alone—appreciating Him for His grace, your faith and your eternal salvation.

Day 20 I Taking Action on following page

"Every good gift and every perfect gift is from above, coming down from the Father of lights, with whom there is no variation or shadow due to change."
James 1:17

<u>Day 20</u>

Taking Action

Please join me in prayer

Heavenly Father, it is good to be reminded of the reality of hell from which you saved us. Together, we acknowledge you as our Savior, and we appreciate you for giving us new life, new perspective and eternal salvation. Thank you, Father, for freeing us from our bondage to sin and from an eternity separated from you. See to it that we steward our salvation well as we seek to glorify you by attaining a grateful heart. In everything, may you receive glory.

We pray in your Son's name, Amen.

Speak to God for a moment appreciating Him
for His grace, your faith and your salvation.
Feel free to write to God, pray silently or pray aloud.

Appreciate God for what He is doing

Appreciate
What He Has Done • **What He Is Doing**
What He Has Yet To Do

A prayer for you today

Jesus, we are thankful for the wisdom you are imparting to us through the inner workings of this book. We are grateful for the spiritual growth developing within us as we seek you with all our heart and mind. Continue to reveal your full worth, and see to it that we display your worthiness to the world. For your glory alone, Amen.

You are more than halfway through this 40 Day Journey with Christ and hopefully by God's grace, Jesus is becoming more satisfying to you with each passing day.

Appreciate what God is doing by sharing what God is doing with others

---

My Personal Revelations

198

Know that the entirety of this book has been written with you in mind. With every stroke of the pen and tap on the keyboard, the desire has been to disciple you by teaching you how to pray and inspiring you to engage in it and live from it. *Is it working? Have you discovered new insights about God that enrich your spiritual walk with Him? Are you desiring God more with each passing day?* If so, appreciate this moment. Appreciate who you are and who you are becoming as you venture through this book with the purpose of knowing and experiencing Jesus!

To know and experience Jesus is your greatest pursuit, and you are intentionally fulfilling your calling. For that, you are appreciated, and you are an inspiration! It's inspiring to know that you for opening yourself up to God and inviting Godly change into your life. *For today's Taking Action, consider sharing with others what you are experiencing. Bless someone with their*

"Therefore encourage one another and build one another up, just as you are doing." 1 Thessalonians 5:11

own copy of TALK TO JESUS and inspire
them with this 40 Day Journey.
Refuse to let your 40 Day Journey end
without equipping someone you know
and love with the same wisdom and
insights you are receiving.

**"Therefore encourage one another and
build one another up, just as you are
doing." 1 Thessalonians 5:11**

It is vital that you build up the body of
Christ and share with other believers the
blessings you receive. Extend the
knowledge and wisdom of God to those
around you and encourage them to seek
God through prayer and through
His Word.

Taking Action

Having an appreciation for God means to
recognize His full worth and align
yourself to display His worthiness.
For today's Taking Action, ask yourself,
"Through twenty days of TALK TO JESUS,

200

have I discovered new insights about God that enrich my spiritual walk with Him? Have I received a new share of God's worthiness, and am I sharing His worthiness with the people around me?"

Christian, every good gift God gives is valuable and worthy to be shared. If you are experiencing a new share of God's worthiness through the inner workings of this book, *share it!*

Write down the names of two people with whom you will share TALK TO JESUS. As a gift, present them with their own copy, or simply enlighten them of its usefulness.

Day 21 I Taking Action on following page

<u>Day 21</u>

Taking Action

Appreciate God for what He is doing by sharing what God is doing with others. Who do you know who might benefit from this book? A family member? A friend? A classmate? A coworker? Your Pastor or another Christian leader?

Write down the names of two people with whom you will share TALK TO JESUS. As a gift, present them with their own copy, or simply enlighten them of its usefulness.

____

Person #1

____

Person #2

TALK TO JESUS is available on Amazon and other online booksellers and at t2j.org.

Once you have completed your 40 Day Journey, consider becoming a Group Leader/Mentor for those who have yet to experience TALK TO JESUS.

22

Appreciate God for what He has yet to do

Appreciate
What He Has Done • What He Is Doing
What He Has Yet To Do

A prayer for you today

Jesus, we present ourselves to you hopeful for a promising future. My friend in Christ and I willingly place our lives in your hands as we trust you to make good on your promises. See to it that we steward well all that you provide, and reward us for our stewardship. We pray in your name, Amen.

God's knowledge and foresight of what is good transcends that of our own, and for this reason, we can appreciate everything God has yet to do because

God's plan for your future is better than any plan you could imagine or dream up

---

My Personal Revelations

____

____

____

____

____

____

____

____

____

____

____

203

we know His plan for our future is better than our plan. Not one of us is able to determine the exact future God has predestined for us while on earth. We live *by faith, through hope.* We cling to the promises set forth by God and develop a trust in Him that produces within us a heart and mind guarded by His divine power.

Believer, God has promised to complete His good work in you and He is able, faithful and willing to make good on His promise. **As a child of God, you are the most treasured person you know! There is no one who has more value or worth than you. You are intensely loved by the God of the universe and your future is in His loving hands.** Appreciate this astounding reality by trusting God with what has yet to come and by living your life in a way that demonstrates His eternal glory.

"And whatever you do, in word or deed, do everything in the name of the Lord

Jesus, giving thanks to God the Father through him." Colossians 3:17

In every moment of your life, present yourself with the attitude of having been bought by the blood of Christ. Allow the reality of Christ's death and resurrection (and all the implications of it) to shape how you think, feel, speak, behave and act. This is the essence of having an appreciation for God.

Taking Action

As you abide in Christ and anticipate God's answer to your prayers, avail yourself to steward well that which He already provides. **Luke 16:10 says, "One who is faithful in a very little, is also faithful in much, and one who is dishonest in a very little is also dishonest in much."** Christian, God will give you more if you prepare yourself to receive more. Preparing to receive more happens by proving yourself able, faithful and willing to responsibly manage what God has already given you.

For today's Taking Action, choose one gift God has entrusted to you that you intend to begin stewarding better as you prepare for a better future. Identify the gift and note how you intend to become more responsible in managing what God already provides.

Increase your time in prayer → In addition to acknowledging God and praying for a filling of one of God's own attributes and for the good of another person, begin appreciating God for what He has done, what He is doing and what He has yet to do during your quality time of prayer. Consider increasing your prayer time to thirty minutes. Also, consider splitting your time of prayer into two or three prayer sessions.

"And whatever you do,
in word or deed, do
everything in the name
of the Lord Jesus, giving
thanks to God the Father
through him."
Colossians 3:17

<u>Day 22</u>

Taking Action

Identify a specific gift God has entrusted to you and note how you intend to become more responsible in managing what God already provides.

God's gift to you:

____

How you intend to steward God's gift more responsibly:

Appreciate God

Appreciate God for giving you life

Gracious God, to you I owe everything. I am alive because of the breath you sustain me with, and I am redeemed because of His life whom you saved me with. Therefore, in every circumstance I will give you thanks; for every gift I will give you praise; with every ability, I will give you glory.

———————

"...even as he chose us in him before the foundation of the world, that we should be holy and blameless before him. In love he predestined us for adoption to himself as sons through Jesus Christ."

Ephesians 1:4-5

———————

REFLECT

In greeting the Church at Ephesus, Paul informs his readers of the eternal love of God and the destiny born to them through the life, death and resurrection of Jesus. In this passage of scripture, Paul illustrates to the church the selective nature of God and the image-bearing responsibility He entrusts to His children.

ABSORB

God specifically chose you, believer in Christ, to bear His image and shine His light onto an unbelieving world. He has wiped out your transgressions and given you eternal life. Appreciate the love, mercy and grace God has poured over you by loving Him back and embracing the responsibility that comes with being chosen.

"...even as he chose us in him before the foundation of the world, that we should be holy and blameless before him. In love he predestined us for adoption to himself as sons through Jesus Christ."
Ephesians 1:4-5

Jesus, it is hard to fathom the eternal love you have for me. I am humbled and grateful knowing you had me in mind even before you spoke the world into being. You knew you wanted me in your family and you paid the ultimate price to adopt me. Help me steward well my relationship with you as I continually choose you as my ultimate satisfaction. **Hear my prayer as I appreciate you...**

"...even as he ___________ us in him before the foundation of the world, that we should be _________ and ___________________ before him. In love he _______________________ us for adoption to himself as sons through Jesus Christ." Ephesians 1:4-5

ADMIT TO GOD

24

Admit Your Sin

Admit
Confess and Repent

A prayer for you today

Jesus, with love, discipline us for our sin. Let us feel the distance our sin causes between us and you, and let your love for us and your desire to fellowship with us inspire us to stop sinning. Amen.

Sin keeps you from experiencing the fullness of God, yet it is the one thing that ought to compel you to seek Him. Sin, in all its wickedness, is essential to your dependency on and your maturity in Christ.

Do you remember the first moments God began to gain your attention? God revealed to you your sin and your need

Sin keeps you from experiencing the fullness of God, yet it is the one thing that ought to compel you to seek Him

---

My Personal Revelations

____

____

____

____

____

____

____

____

____

____

213

for a Savior, and at the same time, God revealed to you His transforming love and satisfying compassion. **And you responded by following Him...** *Why?* Because you realized you were lost and your life outside of God was meaningless. You were made aware of the separation your sin caused between you and God, and in your brokenness, you desired to be healed and saved. In those first moments of sin-awareness, you grieved your sin in such a way that it drove you into the arms of Christ. Christian, ask yourself, *"Does my sin still grieve me the way it once did or do I still practice sin as if God does not live within me? Does my sin still reveal to me my need for an outpouring of God's mercy and grace as it did when I first experienced Jesus?"* Surely, mourning over your sin is not something you do once to receive admission into heaven only to return to your old way of doing things. **Jesus called you to** *follow Him*.

"There is therefore now no condemnation for those who are in Christ Jesus." Romans 8:1

He called you to put on the mind of God daily, so that with it you can judge your life. Throughout the scriptures, God reminds you that your hatred for sin measures your love for Him.

Psalm 97:10 says, "O you who love the LORD, hate evil!"

Do you hate evil? If so, do you hate evil enough to flee from it or do you love it just enough so that it enslaves you? Believer, allow God to examine you for sin as you examine yourself. Admit and repent wherever necessary, receive forgiveness, and refuse to go on sinning.

"If we say we have no sin, we deceive ourselves, and the truth is not in us. If we confess our sins, he is faithful and just to forgive us our sins and cleanse us from all unrighteousness." 1 John 1:8-9

God says all have sinned; if you believe otherwise, the truth is not in you. However, if you acknowledge and confess your sins, repent and ask for forgiveness, God will make you clean.

215

"Work out your own salvation with fear and trembling, for it is God who works in you both to will and to work for his good pleasure." **Philippians 2:12b-13**

To tremble at God's presence is a blessing. Realize that the same God who created and upholds everything in existence also lives inside you and is helping you work out your salvation. When you overcome evil by doing good, it is not your doing, but God's. Likewise, when you overcome temptations by walking according to the Spirit rather than the flesh, it is not your power at work, but God's! God is that close to you and that much for you.
Therefore, tremble at His presence, submit to His power, and join Him in defeating your sin.

"There is therefore now no condemnation for those who are in Christ Jesus." **Romans 8:1**

For all who have received Jesus as their Savior and Lord, the burden of sin no longer has its effect. Every born-again person is fully united with God through the intervention of His Son.

Taking Action

You are no longer a slave to sin. Your old heart, which was enslaved to sin, has been crucified with Christ, and just as Jesus died an earthly death and rose to new life, so did your old heart. The moment you received Jesus, you received a new heart. The *new heart* you hold is governed by the heart and Spirit of Christ, and therefore you are no longer a slave to sin because Christ has set you free.

Allow the reality of this truth to resonate in your mind until you fully realize you are set free from every sin you think you are still enslaved to. You are no longer a slave to sin. You are no longer a slave to fear. **Through Christ, you are a child of God.**

"Work out your own salvation with fear and trembling, for it is God who works in you both to will and to work for his good pleasure."
Philippians 2:12b-13

For today's Taking Action, absorb the truth of God's Word (Galatians 2:20) into your heart and mind as you claim it by speaking it to yourself:

"I am born-again and therefore I am no longer a slave to sin! My old heart has 'been crucified with Christ. It is no longer I who live, but Christ who lives in me. And the life I now live in the flesh I live by faith in the Son of God, who loved me and gave himself for me'."

Galatians 2:20

218

<u>Day 24</u>

Taking Action

Absorb into your heart the reality of this truth
and consider the fruit of your meditation.

"I am born-again and therefore I am no longer a slave to sin! My old heart has 'been crucified with Christ. It is no longer I who live, but Christ who lives in me. And the life I now live in the flesh I live by faith in the Son of God, who loved me and gave himself for me'."
Galatians 2:20

<u>Fruit of your meditation</u>

Admit to God

Admit to God wherein you there is still sin

Lord of Mercy, you became the offering for sin though you knew no sin. Your death on the cross was undeserving, yet you chose to die so I would not perish. Search me for sin, Lord, and discipline me in what you find. Forgive me and cleanse me of my unrighteousness, and see to it that I fulfill your good purpose with my life.

"The LORD is far from the wicked, but he hears the prayer of the righteous." Proverbs 15:29

REFLECT

At the beginning of this passage of scripture, Solomon informs his readers of the distance God imposes between Himself and those who live in defiance to Him. He completes the passage, however, by saying God is attuned to the prayers of those who live according to His Word and practice His righteousness.

220

ABSORB

Solomon's message is written for you as much as it was written to readers of old. Your sin keeps you from experiencing the joy of knowing Jesus. When you sin, you prevent yourself from being filled with the fullness of God and limit what He is willing to provide. However, as you obey the commandments of scripture and live as Jesus lived, your obedience opens the ears of God so that He hears your every prayer.

"The LORD is far from the wicked, but he hears the prayer of the righteous." Proverbs 15:29

Jesus, forgive me for distancing myself from you because of my sin. Discipline me in my distance and see to it that I repent. Fight with me as I resist the devil; and refuse to let up the fight until I have overcome. **Hear my prayer as I admit my sins; and draw near to me as I draw near to you...**

"The LORD is _______ from the wicked, but He ___________ _______ ______________ of the righteous." Proverbs 15:29

ASK GOD

Fast

List a God-given passion you regularly enjoy and plan a specific time
to fast from this passion on one occasion over the next three days.
During your time of fasting, have a purpose for your fast.

Your God-Given Passion (e.g. Favorite hobby or activity):

*Specified Time of Fasting (e.g. A specific time [1-2 hours] on
Day 27 when you would otherwise be enjoying a favorite
hobby or activity):*

Your Purpose For Fasting:
(see page 166 for a list of examples)

Ask God

Ask
**Eternal Regenerative Petitions
Kingdom-Minded Temporal Petitions**

A prayer for you today

Jesus, we are delighted to speak with you and be heard. Our greatest desire is to align our desires with yours and receive your response to our prayers. Teach us how we ought to ask of you, and give us proper motive so that our prayers honor you and bring you glory. Amen.

When asking of God, always desire for God to receive the glory. In His Word, God says, **"Whatever you ask in my name I will do, that the *Father may be glorified in the Son*. If you ask me anything in my name, I will do it"** John 14:13-14.

When asking of God, always desire for God to receive the glory

---

My Personal Revelations

____

____

____

____

____

____

____

____

____

____

____

225

God's response to your prayers is for your eternal good and ultimately for His eternal glory. When you ask of God, your heart should say to Him, "My greatest desire is for you to glorify yourself in your response to my prayer." That is, every prayer you pray should honor God as it arises from your humble state of dependence and reliance upon Him.

If you pray a prayer and do not desire for the *Father to be glorified* but rather seek to advance your personal agenda, it is not a God-honoring prayer.

The most God-honoring prayers look like this: "God if you can receive glory for yourself and your kingdom can advance by prospering me in any measure and in any way, then so be it; but dear God if your kingdom will advance and your name will be glorified through me being ground to powder, then so be it."

Paul Washer, American Christian Evangelist; Sermon titled "God's Man"

Believer, "prayer does not exist as a means of control whereby you attempt to force God's hand for the promotion, advancement or even the preservation of yourself" (Paul Washer, *God's Man*). Rather, prayer is the communication between a dependent child and an independent God. God alone is in control, and through prayer He invites you to join Him in carrying out His plan for your life and all of creation.

There are two types of petitions: **Eternal Regenerative Petitions and Kingdom-Minded Temporal Petitions.**

Eternal Regenerative Petitions *is a petitioning of God for a greater measure of His regenerative qualities so that you conform to the likeness of Christ and glorify God in the way you think, feel, speak, behave and act.*
There is nothing more satisfying to God than to hear your heart petition Him for a continual outpouring and filling of His own attributes. Likewise, no greater aim is there for which you live.

"You do not have, because you do not ask." James 4:2b

227

Kingdom-Minded Temporal Petitions *is asking God to fulfill His every promise by providing for you all that is necessary to carry out His will so that His kingdom advances and the love of Christ is shared.*

God has designed you with specific needs so you would rely on Him to have your needs met. And in the process of having your needs met, God desires to be glorified by receiving praise from you and those around you.

Note that when you pray for your needs and the needs of others, your main purpose for praying should not center on you or another person being healed, prospered or even preserved. Rather, your prayers should arise from your desire for God to be glorified, Jesus to be worshiped and for the kingdom of heaven to advance.

Asking of God in this manner will ensure that you receive everything you ask for.

"You do not have, because
you do not ask." James 4:2b

Often you do not receive from God simply because you do not ask for it.

"You ask and do not receive, because you ask wrongly, to spend it on your passions." James 4:3

God wants to answer "yes" to your prayers. He wants to reward you so that your joy remains full. However, if you ask of God with improper motives, He will say no. Never force God's hand in attempt to glorify yourself.

"Therefore do not be anxious, saying, 'What will we eat?' or 'What will we drink?' or 'What will we wear?' For the Gentiles seek after all these things, and your heavenly Father knows that you need them all. But seek first the kingdom of God and his righteousness, and all these things will be added to you." Matthew 6:31-33

God is always good on His promise.
Trust God to fulfill His promises to you as
you focus your heart and mind on who
He is and the power He has,
rather than fearing you will not be
provided for.

Taking Action

There is a reason the Holy Spirit resides in you. Holy Spirit is a wise Counselor who is mediating the conflict happening between your sinful flesh and your regenerated soul. He has taken root in your heart and continually speaks to God on your behalf—pleading with God to feed into your heart and mind the wisdom and knowledge of the scriptures. Moment by moment, Holy Spirit is weaning you off your former way of thinking and doing things as He leads you into faith and repentance.

All of this is His job.

The Holy Spirit cannot do His job however, without cooperation from you.

230

The underlying principle that permits spiritual transformation is your willingness to submit to the righteous governance of the Holy Spirit. It is only through submission to Him (Holy Spirit) that you allow God to complete His good work in you and through you. Understand that when you pray God's will, Holy Spirit is praying, not you. Likewise, when you repent, Holy Spirit is repenting, *not you.* And when your faith is expressed through good works, it is the Holy Spirit's doing, not yours. In all this, you are simply yielding to the Holy Spirit, and allowing Him to pray, repent and complete His good work in you.

Today's Taking Action has two parts. Part one invites you to engage the righteousness of God made available to you through His Holy Spirit. That is, in addition to the one attribute for which you have been praying, begin asking God to let flow from you *every attribute* of the Holy Spirit. Do so by speaking the attributes of God's Spirit (love, joy, peace, patience, kindness, goodness, gentleness, faithfulness, self-control) into your mind and into your heart. Spend an even greater amount of time in prayer petitioning God for each attribute of His Spirit until your heart and mind identifies with and becomes fully aligned with the heart and mind of God.

Part two of today's Taking Action invites you to receive the promises of God by speaking God's Word to your own soul until His promises govern your life. God has promised to meet your physical and spiritual needs according to His good will and good measure. There is not a need God has given you that He has not promised to meet in due season. Avail yourself to the promises of God by speaking them back to God *and to yourself*. In doing so, you will assure yourself of all God has promised and prevent yourself from feeling as if God does not answer your prayers.
He already has.

"You ask and do not receive, because you ask wrongly, to spend it on your passions." James 4:3

<u>Day 26</u>

Taking Action

<u>Part One</u>

Increase your prayer time → In addition to the one attribute of God's Spirit for which you have been praying, commit to seeking *every* attribute of the Holy Spirit. Begin today by spending additional time with God in prayer reflecting upon and absorbing each of His attributes into your heart and mind until everything you are is everything God is.

Attributes of the Holy Spirit

Love, Joy, Peace, Patience, Kindness,

Goodness, Gentleness, Faithfulness, Self-Control

<u>Part Two</u>

Using *Jesus' Model Prayer* as an example, we see three needs common to humanity. With each of these needs we also see throughout scripture God's promise to provide:

1. "Give us each day our daily bread." Luke 11:3

   • **"And my God will supply every need of yours according to his riches in glory in Christ Jesus." Philippians 4:19**

2. "Forgive us our debts, as we have also forgiven our debtors."
Luke 11:4

   - **"If we confess our sins, he is faithful and just to forgive us our sins and to cleanse us from all unrighteousness."**
   1 John 1:9

3. "Lead us not into temptation but deliver us from evil."
Matthew 6:13

   - **"No temptation has overtaken you that is not common to man. God is faithful, and he will not let you be tempted beyond your ability, but with the temptation he will also provide the way of escape, that you may be able to endure it." 1 Corinthians 10:13**

Take action by acknowledging the promises of God found in scripture. Proclaim these promises God has made by speaking them back to God *and to yourself* until they govern the way you think, feel, speak, behave and act.

Writing space is available for you on the following page to list, seek and absorb the attributes of God's Spirit. Additional writing space is provided for you on page 236 to write, reflect upon and absorb the aforementioned promises of God found in scripture.

234

Attributes of the Holy Spirit

___________________, ___________________, ___________________

___________________, ___________________, ___________________

___________________, ___________________, ___________________

Ask God for a filling of every attribute that defines Christ

Philippians 4:19

1 John 1:9

1 Corinthians 10:13

**Speak the promises of God back to God until He makes good on
His every promise. Likewise, speak the promises of God to yourself
until His promises govern your life.**

27

Ask God

Eternal Regenerative Petitions

Ask God to fill you with the love of Christ

My Father, create in me a pure heart, and renew in me a right spirit.
Rid me of my selfish ways and restore me with the joy of your
salvation. Anoint and fill me with your Holy Spirit;
make way for Him to take root and produce within me the seeds
that bear much fruit.

---

*"Anyone who does not love does not know God,
because God is love." 1 John 4:8*

REFLECT

In writing to Christians, the apostle John communicates to his readers
the evidence that declares their righteousness. John reveals to them
the significance of love and the proof of salvation it provides.

ABSORB

Love is the one attribute of the Holy Spirit that binds every other attribute together in perfect harmony. The character of God's Spirit is perfected in you when you love God and love other people. As you pray today, ask God to remove from within you impatience, pride, selfishness, anger and bitterness and to fill you with a love that is patient, humble, giving, gentle and forgiving.

*"Anyone who does not love does not know God,
because God is love." 1 John 4:8*

God, I want to know you. If to know you is to love and to love is to know you, love is all I need. Pour your Spirit over me and fill me with a love that is patient, humble, giving, gentle and forgiving.
Father, glorify yourself in me in your response to my asking...

PRAYER SESSION | ASK GOD

____

____

____

____

____

____

____

____

____

____

____

____

____

____

____

"Anyone who does not _________ does not know _______,

because _______ ____ _________."

1 John 4:8

Ask God

Kingdom Minded Temporal Petitions

Ask God to fulfill His promises

My God, you are able to provide, faithful to provide and willing to provide according to your good purpose. Fulfill your promises to me so that in you alone I am satisfied.

"Seek first the Kingdom of God and His righteousness, and all these things will be added to you." Matthew 6:33

REFLECT

In this passage of scripture, Matthew quotes the words of Jesus. In His Sermon on the Mount, Jesus tells His hearers to consider a higher spiritual life; that is, consider it more valuable to seek God than to be consumed by the anxieties of seeking worldly gain.

ABSORB

When you ask of God, always have His kingdom in mind. Through

240

Matthew 6:33, Jesus is saying to you, "Consider me above every care, concern and worry. Keep your eyes fixated on me and chase after my righteousness, and I will meet every need and desire you have."

As you pray today, ask God to meet your every need and desire according to His good will and good measure, bearing in mind your ultimate purpose for praying is for God to receive glory and honor and praise.

"Seek first the Kingdom of God and His righteousness, and all these things will be added to you." Matthew 6:33

God, I trust that you have my best interest in mind. Give to me only that which brings you glory and causes your kingdom to advance. If you can receive glory by prospering me in any measure and in any way, so be it; but dear God if you will receive glory in giving me less than my heart's desire, let your will be done. I will follow you no matter the prosperity or the cost.

Provide for me according to your good will as I ask you to meet my needs and accomplish my heart's desires...

242

"Seek first the _______________ ____ _______ and His righteousness,

and _______ these things will be added to you." Matthew 6:33

ADVOCATE

Advocate For Others

Advocate

Intercede on behalf of other people

A prayer for you today

Jesus, we are grateful to have people in our lives we can relate to. Inspire us as we take interest in the lives of other people and avail ourselves to their life story. Develop within us a passion to invest our prayers, our time and our energy into bringing out the good in our fellow man. Amen.

There is nothing God desires more than for you to love people with the same measure of love you have for yourself and Him. To love God means to love people, and often your love for another person is demonstrated by the amount

The amount of time you spend interceding for others is a testimony to the love you have for them

My Personal Revelations

247

of time you spend interceding for them. Every person has significant worth and a story to tell, and God calls you to avail yourself to the unfolding story of another person's life by taking an interest in them. Going forward, determine to pour your heart out to God in support of other people as you walk beside them through life. In doing so, take pleasure in knowing that your commitment to pray for people is the most impactful gift you can give them.

"Do nothing from selfish ambition or conceit, but in humility count others more significant than yourselves. Let each of you look not only to his own interests, but also to the interests of others." Philippians 2:3-4

Remind yourself daily that you are created to relate with other people— *to rejoice in their blessings, share their burdens and pray for them always.* Make it your mission to become an

"First of all, then, I urge that supplications, prayers, intercessions and thanksgivings be made for all people."
1 Timothy 2:1

DAY 29 | ADVOCATE FOR OTHERS

inspirational character in the storybook of another person's life.

"First of all, then, I urge that supplications, prayers, intercessions, and thanksgivings be made for all people." _1 Timothy 2:1_

God wills that you petition Him to prevent evil, procure good and provide grace and mercy to all people. The prayers of the righteous have power, and God desires to hear from you on behalf of your fellow brothers and sisters, as well as the unsaved.

Taking Action

An important part of prayer is your willingness to become part of the answer.

Christian, in as much as you pray for another person, act upon that which you pray. Come alongside of people and allow the Holy Spirit who is alive within you to gain their attention.

For today's Taking Action, be encouraged to reach out to the person for whom you have been praying these past four weeks. Let them know you have been praying for them and *tell them why*. Also, consider the ways you can come alongside this person as you work with God to become the answer to your intercessory prayers.

<u>Day 29</u>

Taking Action

Reach out to the person for whom you have been praying. Tell them why you have been praying for them and consider the ways you can become the answer to your prayers.

Using the writing space provided, jot down steps you can take toward becoming the answer to your prayers for this person, *and then become the answer!* Also, consider using this space to journal the response this person gave once you told him or her that you have been praying on their behalf.

Advocate For Others

<u>Prayer Session</u>

**Ask God to enrich others with an empowered spiritual walk,
spiritual wisdom and strength through weakness**

Father, turn your ear to my intercessions for my fellow man. Grant
them eternal salvation and spiritual wisdom for your heavenly glory.
Fulfill your provisional promises in each of their lives and see to it that
they present themselves to you having been conformed to Christ's
deity on the Day of Judgment.

---

*"Let each of you look not only to his own interests, but also to the
interests of others." Philippians 2:4*

REFLECT

In this passage of scripture, the Apostle Paul encourages his Christian
readers to consider the welfare of other people as they do their own.
Paul encourages Christians to gain insight into the thoughts, hopes
and aspirations of other people by taking an interest in them.

253

ABSORB

In your prayers as well as your actions, consider the well-being of other people. Develop a mindset that not only seeks after your own interests, but seeks the interests of others as well. Get to know a person's spiritual walk, their spiritual wisdom and their needs, temptations and desires. Pray for them as you come alongside of them in action and in truth.

"Let each of you look not only to his own interests, but also to the interests of others." Philippians 2:4

God, give power to my prayer as I plead with you on behalf of other people. Give me a profound interest in their well-being so I can work together with you to see that your will for each of their lives unfolds. **Hear my prayer as I advocate on behalf of others...**

"Let _________ of you look not only to his own ___________________,
but also to the interests of _____________." Philippians 2:4

31

Final Acknowledgement

Acknowledge His Glory Alone

A prayer for you today

Jesus, above all, we desire to honor you in the way we think, speak, behave and act. Our earnest prayers derive from our passion to be changed by you and for you; for you alone are worthy to be worshiped and praised. In everything, see to it that your name is glorified. Amen.

Through prayer, your hopes are alive because God is able, faithful and willing to fulfill His promises as you call on Him in truth and righteousness. Prayer enables you to experience the joy of having just spoken with the God of the universe, and that joy you receive from

Rejoice in knowing your ultimate purpose for praying is not to glorify yourself, but to bring glory to God

---

My Personal Revelations

____

____

____

____

____

____

____

____

____

____

256

Him ought to produce within you contentment for whatever God's response to your prayer is. Throughout history, God has proven Himself trustworthy and unchanging, and for this reason you can confidently say "Amen!" knowing God is faithful and willing to respond to you with your best interest in mind.

"And we know that for those who love God all things work together for good, for those who are called according to his purpose." Romans 8:28

Above all, rejoice in knowing your ultimate purpose for praying is not to glorify yourself, but to bring glory to the Savior of your soul, the Lord of your life and the One who has a greater plan for you than you could ever imagine or dream up.

"In the same way, let your light shine before others, so that they may see your

"So whether you eat or drink, or whatever you do, do it all for the glory of God." 1 Corinthians 10:31

good works and give glory to your

Father who is in heaven."

Matthew 5:16

The measure of faith and righteousness
you receive comes solely from God.
Therefore, every good work produced by
your faith should be done for the glory
and praise of God only.

"Whatever you ask in my name, this I
will do, that the Father may be glorified
in the Son." John 14:13

Everything you do, in word or deed,
should be done in the name of Jesus so
that the Father receives glory from
what His Son does.

Taking Action

"So whether you eat or drink, or
whatever you do, do it all for the glory
of God." 1 Corinthians 10:31

258

Christian, God's glory shines through you when you think, speak and act in a manner that reveals to the world just how glorious God is. When you trust God above everything else, you reveal to the world the glory of His trustworthiness. Likewise, when you choose to remain satisfied in Him no matter your situation or circumstance, you reveal to the world God's satisfying nature and thirst-quenching power. **This is the aim of your life—*to reveal to the world the glory of God!***

For today's Taking Action, be conscious of your every thought, word, feeling and action, and ask yourself:
- *"Does this glorify God?"*
- *"Do my thoughts honor God and make Him look glorious?"*
- *"Does my speech give grace to those who hear?"*
- *"Does the way I feel reveal my faith and declare my satisfaction in Christ?"*

- *"Does the way I act cause other people to see Jesus and desire to know Him?"*

Believer, you are created to image God so that through you, the world will see His glory. This is your purpose and your worth, and there is no greater worth than this.

Day 31

Taking Action

Be conscious of your every thought, word, feeling and action, and ask yourself: "Does this glorify God?" "Do my thoughts honor God?" "Does my speech give grace to those who hear?" "Does the way I feel reveal my faith?" "Does the way I act cause other people to see Jesus and desire to know Him?"

Avail yourself to the power of the Holy Spirit and be the image of God today and every day.

PRAYER AS A DISPOSITION

**Prayer As A Disposition calls for a day break in the
40 Day Journey**

**Treat Prayer As A Disposition as a 'day' wherein you
consider what it means to *pray without ceasing***

PRAYER AS A DISPOSITION

PRAYING WITHOUT CEASING

Everything you have read, experienced and acted upon thus far has amounted to this moment. Today is not numbered. It is not one of the 40 days. Rather, it is all 40 days in one. Making prayer the disposition of your life is your final destination.

Said by Leonard Ravenhill, a visionary evangelist who focused on the subjects of prayer and revival: "If there is any prayer that needs to be prayed in the church of God today, it is 'Lord, teach us to pray'. Not teach us to *want* to pray, teach us *to pray*! Teach us what it is—not the vocabulary, but the disposition. Prayer is not latitude, but an attitude! Prayer is not a position on your face or knees; prayer is a disposition. That is why Paul said it is possible to get to that point where you *pray without ceasing*; where every moment of your life you are in an attitude of relationship to Jesus—*not for something you want!* But so God might come again and somehow breathe."

Christian, prayer is a disposition cultivated through intimate heartfelt communication with God. Your time spent alone with God in prayer enables Him to transform the disposition of your heart by renewing the condition of your mind. The more intimate you become with God through quality time spent alone with Him, the greater your satisfaction will be in everything God is and everything God does. **Intimacy with God is the cause for praying without ceasing.**

To pray without ceasing is to be in an attitude of relationship to Jesus every moment of every day. Put another way, to pray without ceasing is to have a heart that has been so transformed by God that it approaches and responds to every situation and circumstance as God would.

It is important to note that this type of praying (praying without ceasing) does not happen overnight; rather, it is something you approximate to. It emerges as your love for God grows and rises as you become more obedient to His Word.

Prayer as a disposition looks like this: **It approaches life with humility and with a spirit of dependency on its Creator. It is eager to do what is good, even when good is not done to it. It finds something to rejoice in even when it is experiencing some form of suffering or injustice. It gives thanks for everything and for everyone in every circumstance. It admits when it is wrong and immediately begins to fix what has not yet been made right. It forgives without question or thought; its forgiveness is automatic. It is not concerned solely with itself but also for the welfare of others. It loves God and would do anything to make His love known to the world.**

Believer, do you desire to pray without ceasing? Do you aspire to impact the world by taking hold of an unceasing prayer life as described above? If your heart cries out "yes!" to these questions, and your desire is to become so close to God that you are in constant communion with Him every moment of every day, then the Word of God **must** reside in you and manifest itself through you.

As mentioned on Day 2 of this 40 Day Journey, **prayer and the Word of God are inseparably joined.** Prayer cannot function optimally unless it is born out of God's Word, and God's Word cannot do its job of producing faith and fruit without being accompanied by prayer. For this reason, in addition to spending quality time with God in heartfelt prayer, you must memorize, meditate on and respond obediently to the Word of God. Only by memorizing and meditating on the truths found in scripture and responding to them with faith and obedience, will you be able to adopt the mind of God and thus bear His perfect image.

In response to being asked *"How do we learn to pray,"* American Christian evangelist Paul Washer says, "Read the scriptures. Read the commands of scripture. Read the Word of God in scripture. Read 'who is God' in scripture. And read the *prayers* of scripture. Read them, meditate on them, and study them so that you cultivate or develop the mind of Christ—saturating your life in the Word of God until it begins to take over—so that you begin to think like God thinks and speak like Christ spoke."

Throughout the remainder of this 40 Day Journey and beyond, seek to embody an attitude of prayer every moment of every day. Do so by engaging the Word of God until it transforms the way you think, feel, speak and act. Do so by remaining steadfast in your quality time with God as you dialogue with Him through the six A's of prayer. And do so by determining to allow everything you have read and experienced thus far to fulfill its good purpose of empowering you to pray without ceasing.

ABIDING IN GOD'S WORD

Abiding in God's Word

Abiding in God's Word through

Memorization • Meditation • Response

A prayer for you today

Jesus, prepare our minds to receive your Word and the insights your Word provokes. Instill in us a passion for memorizing scripture and grant us the desire to feed on it and live from it. Renew our minds as you develop within us a heart that emulates yours.
We pray in your name, Amen.

Joshua 1:8 says, *"This Book of the Law shall not depart from your mouth, but you shall meditate on it day and night, so that you may be careful to do according to all that is written in it. For then you will make your way*

Accompanied by prayer, memorizing scripture enables you to speak to and hear from God wherever you go

---

My Personal Revelations

____

____

____

____

____

____

____

____

____

____

____

269

prosperous, and then you will have good success."

There are times during the day when it is not possible for you to be reading the Bible. Therefore, to keep God's Word always on your mind and meditate on it day and night, memorization is necessary.

Accompanied by prayer, memorizing scripture enables you to speak to and hear from God wherever you go. As you determine to commit God's Word to memory, your thoughts suddenly become God's thoughts and your actions become that of God's. And the result is you emulating Jesus.

Consider the following passages of scripture:

"I tell you, on the day of judgment people will give account for every careless word they speak, for by your words you will be justified, and by your words you will be condemned."

Matthew 12:36-37

"I, the LORD search the heart and examine the mind, to reward each person according to their conduct, according to what their deeds deserve."
Jeremiah 17:10

Recognize that most of what you do in life (be it your everyday choices or your daily interactions with the world and the people in it) happens without any deep discerning thought. Much of your lifespan is spent acting and reacting to situations and circumstances solely based upon your state of mind and the condition of your heart. For this reason, it is imperative that your heart and mind be renewed and transformed by God, *through His Word*. God's Word trains, corrects, rebukes and teaches you to live your life based on Godly principles rather than your feelings, circumstances and worldly knowledge. Having your heart and mind transformed by the Word of God keeps you from living life

"Let us not love in word or talk, but in deed and truth."
1 John 3:18

by the impulsive nature of your flesh and enables you to bring a good account to God on the Day of Judgment.

Examine your heart.

Luke 6:45 says, *"The good person out of the good treasure of his heart produces good, and the evil person out of his evil treasure produces evil, for out of the abundance of the heart his mouth speaks."*

What is your heart full of? Is it full of God's Word or is it full of the world's wisdom? Is your heart being conditioned to carry out God's will or is it conditioned to carry out your own?

Be inspired to welcome God's Word into your mind, and allow it to penetrate your heart until it transforms your soul. Be encouraged today and each day going forward to memorize and meditate on the knowledge and wisdom of God so that you are empowered to live as God lives and do as God does.

272

How to do it:

Countless practices exist for memorizing scripture. One easy-to-use method for memorizing scripture is the **Rule of 10's.**

The Rule of 10's consists of:

Reading a passage of scripture 10 times

Reciting a passage of scripture 10 times

Taking Action

For today's Taking Action, memorize 1 John 3:18 by reading it ten times and then reciting it ten times. Consider using this technique to memorize and retain many of the more than 30,000 passages of scripture that fill the Bible!

Note → In your daily reading of God's Word, consider what God is saying to you and determine the passages of scripture you desire to commit to memory.

<u>Day 32</u>

Taking Action

Memorize the following passage of scripture by reading it
ten times and then reciting it ten times.
Check off each open space as you read and recite 1 John 3:18.

"Let us not love in word or talk, but in deed and truth."

1 John 3:18

                   Read   **Recite**

1) _________ _________

2) _________ _________

3) _________ _________

4) _________ _________

5) _________ _________

6) _________ _________

7) _________ _________

8) _________ _________

9) _________ _________

10) _________ _________

33

Abiding in God's Word

Abiding in God's Word through

Memorization • **Meditation** • Response

A prayer for you today

Jesus, your Word is alive and well. Through your Word you are working in us and through us to fulfill your good purpose on earth. Establish a connection between your Word and our minds as we meditate on all you have said. See to it that we adopt your language and speak back to you your words of truth in the way we live. Amen.

"The reason we often come away cold from reading God's Word is because we don't warm ourselves by the fire of meditation."

Thomas Watson

Your faith strengthens and your wisdom increases when you meditate on God's Word

My Personal Revelations

275

Before we unveil biblical meditation, it is important to note that not everyone views meditation the same. Many view meditation as a practice designed to help empty the human mind of every thought and to essentially cause the mind to go blank. Biblical meditation is quite the opposite. Rather than voiding the mind of information and thought processes, biblical meditation is the practice of filling the mind with the wisdom and knowledge of God, whereby enabling Godly wisdom to permeate everything in you that is not of God. The mind of God is written in the Word of God, and when you reflect upon and absorb God's Word into your mind, your viewpoint becomes likened to God's viewpoint on everything. Meditating on God's Word awakens you to His eternal perspective, attunes your heart to His will and serves as the gateway to having your prayers answered. Biblical meditation is the pathway to a more intimate experience with God, and your

276

faith strengthens and your wisdom increases as you meditate on God's Word.

Consider the following passage of scripture:

"If you abide in me, and my words abide in you, ask whatever you wish, and it will be done for you." John 15:7

Having God's Word abiding in you is essential to receiving a "yes" response from God regarding your prayers. The evidence of *God's Word abiding* is that it produces within you the fruit of faith and obedience. That is, it actively dwells in your heart and mind, transforming the way you interact with the world and the people in it.

This supernatural happening of heart and mind transformation occurs as you avail yourself to biblical meditation. Therefore, determine to carefully meditate on God's Word day and night. In doing so, a bond between your heart, mind and will and the heart, mind and will of God begins to form. And once God's will begins to form and His character traits become rooted into the core of who you are—renewal, transformation and change will occur.

How to do it:

Meditation on God's Word happens in two phases:

Reflection and Absorption

(previously noted on Day 10)

To Reflect on God's Word means *to think deeply about why the Word was written, what was the author's intent, how God's Word shaped the world at that time and what effect His Word had on the people to whom it was written.*

To Absorb God's Word then, means *to allow what God is saying to you to penetrate your mind until your thoughts, attitude and actions conform to that of Jesus'.*

278

<u>Taking Action</u>

Beneath every key passage of scripture there is a certain depth that is alive and worthy of producing transformation. When you read a passage of scripture, be aware there is always more to see than the words alone. God is not asleep; He and His Word are active and well. God is always presently working through His Word, manifesting Himself in and through His children by way of their careful meditation on what He is saying. For today's Taking Action, meditate on the passage of scripture you memorized on Day 32 by reflecting on what God is saying as you absorb His words into your mind. Allow your mind to linger on specific words or groupings of words until the entire passage of scripture is born into and enlivens your heart. Once God's Word has taken root in your mind and heart, jot down 3-4 revelations that arise as the fruit of your biblical meditation.

"If you abide in me, and my words abide in you, ask whatever you wish, and it will be done for you."
John 15:7

279

Note → Provided for you below is a biblical context and commentary of 1 John 3:18 so you can reflect upon and absorb this verse into your mind and heart.

<u>Day 33</u>

Taking Action

Meditate on the passage of scripture you memorized on Day 32 by reflecting on God's Word and absorbing it into your heart and mind. Once your heart and mind identifies with the heart and mind of Christ, use the writing space provided on page 282 to jot down 3-4 revelations that arise as the fruit of your mediation.

"Let us not love in word or talk, but in deed and truth."
1 John 3:18

REFLECT

In this passage of scripture, the Apostle John is telling his Christian readers to not sit idle. He reminds them of what it means to truly love God and love people—that is, to *love in action!*

"If anyone has the world's goods and sees his brother in need, yet closes his heart against him, how does God's love abide in him?" 1 John 3:17

Notice the passage of scripture (verse 17) that precedes the passage of scripture you memorized on Day 32 (verse 18). Through His Word in 1 John 3:17-18, God is beckoning you to take specific types of action.

He is asking you to step out of the comforts of your own securities and selfish life plan and to become richly involved in the lives of other people. God is asking you to be generous with your time and money, to stand for those who cannot stand for themselves, to fight against injustice, show mercy, display grace and love in action.

As you meditate on 1 John 3:18, allow God's Word to abide in you and inspire you to love people with the true love of God—
a love demonstrated by taking action.

"Let us not love in word or talk, but in deed and truth."
1 John 3:18

Fruit of your Meditation

What is God saying to you personally through 1 John 3:18

34

Abiding in God's Word

Abiding in God's Word through

Memorization • Meditation • **Response**

A prayer for you today

Jesus, you are the image of God whom
we desire to image. In your obedience,
you became a man to reveal to us
the Father and to teach us how to live.
Empower us to emulate you as we seek
to respond to your Word with faith and
obedience. Through every good deed,
let your name alone be glorified.
Amen.

When the Word of God abides in you, it
is at work within you—renewing your
mind and transforming your heart as
you interact with it by responding to it.
Giving response to God's Word is the

**Responding to God's Word
is the spark that activates
God's power to complete
His good work in you and
through you**

My Personal Revelations

spark that activates God's power to complete His good work in you and through you. Responding to the Word of God causes you to grow and results in the Holy Spirit producing within you the fruit that advances God's kingdom.

Responding to God's Word is accomplished in four ways:

1. Respond dependently

2. Respond obediently

3. Respond appreciatively

4. Respond confidently

Respond Dependently

Respond dependently to God's Word because without it there is no transformation. Without the Word of God, there is no means for discernment, no promises of provision and no regenerative hope. You must rely on the Word of God to be confident in the will of God and to remain faithful to Him.

284

Respond Obediently

Respond to God's Word with obedience because there is no substitute. God has made known what He approves of, and it is both your privilege and your responsibility to be transformed by the Word of God through your obedience to it.

Respond Appreciatively

Respond to God's Word appreciatively knowing that the faith and fruit that God's Word produces in you and through you comes solely from God and not from your human effort.

Respond Confidently

Respond to God's Word with confidence knowing that your dead soul has been restored and is being made fully alive to Christ as the Word of God abides in you. Be confident knowing that the Word that abides in you has transforming power and is conforming your heart and mind to the heart and mind of Jesus.

<u>Taking Action</u>

God wrote a library of 66 interrelated books we call the Bible. He wrote these books for us to know, trust and enjoy Him for who He truly is. He also wrote them so we would know who we are in relationship to Him and to provide for us the means of knowing how we ought to respond to Him as a sinner and as a saint.

For today's taking action, respond to the passage of scripture you memorized and meditated upon these past two days. Respond to God's Word by putting His Word into action so that through you it does its job of revealing God's glory for everyone to see.

Note → Provided for you is a *Life Message* (a practical way to apply God's Word) to reveal to you how you might respond to and enact 1 John 3:18.

286

<u>Day 34</u>

Taking Action

Respond to the passage of scripture you memorized and meditated upon these past two days. Respond to God's Word by putting it into action so that through you it does its job of revealing God's glory for everyone to see.

"Let us not love in word or talk, but in deed and truth."
1 John 3:18

Life Message

Many of us hold to a false sense of love. We view love as an attraction and an emotion rather than an action and a behavior. We get quite good at saying, *"I love you"*, but lag at putting *"I love you"* into action. **The truth is—love is something you do, not just something you say or feel. Love may produce an emotion, but love requires action.** As you respond to 1 John 3:18, consider the actions you can take to demonstrate the love of God back to God, to yourself and to people.

Ask yourself, *"How might I demonstrate the love of God back to God in the way I act toward Him? How might I demonstrate the love of God in the way I think, speak, behave and act toward myself and others?"*

Feel free to use the writing space below to list action steps you plan to take to reveal God's love back to God, to yourself and to others. In your future, refer to your notes below as a reminder to always demonstrate God's love by taking action.

How I can love in action toward...

God: ____

____

____

____

____

____

____

____

____

____

____

____

____

____

____

Myself:

Others:

It has been an incredible journey.

Throughout these 40 days you have invited God in and allowed Him to transform your life. You have met with God through prayer, memorized and meditated on His Word and responded to Him by taking action.

You have followed the will of God.

Now it is time to finish the race.

The Apostle Paul once wrote:

"I am not saying that I have this all together, or that I have it made. But I am well on my way, reaching out for Christ, who has so wondrously reached out for me… I've got my eye on the goal, where God is beckoning us onward – to Jesus. I am off and running, and I am not turning back." Philippians 3:12-14 (MSG)

Christian, let this passage of scripture inspire you to continue seeking Christ with the same fervency you have sought Him with throughout this 40 Day Journey. Days 35 through 40 are solely committed to enabling you to TALK TO JESUS. Each day is titled with an *Attitudinal Truth* (a particular attitude/mindset worth developing) and a relevant *Life Message* to encourage you to follow God's will long after these 40 days have passed.

To you, brothers and sisters in Christ:

Allow your dialogue with God to become the disposition of your life as you seek to always be in an attitude of relationship to Jesus.

35

Approach life with the joyous satisfaction that comes through knowing Jesus

Gracious Lord, I present myself ready to hear your Word and ready to receive from you a revelation. In you I place my confidence. In you I put my trust. In you I am absolutely satisfied.

"Jesus said to them, I am the bread of life; whoever comes to me shall not hunger, and whoever believes in me shall never thirst."
John 6:35

Life Message

"God is most glorified in you when you are most satisfied in Him."
– John Piper

In every situation and circumstance, seek and find the satisfaction that comes through knowing and experiencing Jesus. Have a cheerful regard for anything and everything that comes your way, especially when difficulties challenge you. Finding satisfaction in God during moments of hardship makes God look most glorious, as it proves to the world God's ability to satisfy even amid pain and suffering. Believer, throughout every happening, good or bad, remain consciously aware of God's everlasting love and satisfying nature— reminding yourself daily that you are *new* and cared for.

"Jesus said to them, I am the bread of life; whoever comes to me shall not hunger, and whoever believes in me shall never thirst."
John 6:35

Jesus, I present myself to you *satisfied* because there is nothing more satisfying than to know and experience you. You provide for my every need, and you answer my prayers. You are my rock, my strength, my hope and my purpose.

Hear my words of humility. Hear my grateful heart. Hear my expression of confidence, and draw near to me as I approach you with a desire to experience your presence...

"Jesus said to them, I am the ______________ ______ __________; whoever comes to me shall ________ ________________, and whoever believes in me shall ______________ ________________." John 6:35

Exalt God above every other person and thing

My Father in heaven, you alone are sacred and set apart. You are the Creator of all things and you sustain all you created. You had no beginning, and you will have no end. You are the all-knowing, omnipresent God who has made Himself known.

You are the essence of love, and you have chosen to reside in me.

"Therefore God has highly exalted him and bestowed on him the name that is above every name, so that at the name of Jesus every knee should bow, in heaven and on earth and under the earth, and every tongue confess that Jesus Christ is Lord, to the glory of God the Father." Philippians 2:9-11

Life Message

Elevating Jesus above every other person and thing in your life will cause you discomfort. It will cause you to question the ways of the world and in response, the world will begin to question you.

296

As you choose to exalt Jesus, no longer will you enjoy the comfort of simply fitting in, rather you will be forced to embrace the hardships of standing out. *Are you willing to go there? Are you willing to elevate Jesus above your comfort and above your worldly passions and desires?* On the authority of God's Word, know this:
If you will delight in Christ and exalt Him above every other person and thing in your life, He will come alongside you and produce within you a sense of peace and joy that you will not find anywhere else.

"Therefore God has highly exalted him and bestowed on him the name that is above every name, so that at the name of Jesus every knee should bow, in heaven and on earth and under the earth, and every tongue confess that Jesus Christ is Lord, to the glory of God the Father." Philippians 2:9-11

Jesus, you have chosen to save me and adopt me into your family. Give me courage to acknowledge and exalt you no matter the persecution I face or discomfort I feel.
Become the supreme treasure of my life as I acknowledge you for who you truly are...

297

298

"Therefore God has _______________ ________________ him and bestowed on him the name that is ___________ every name, so that at the name of ___________ every knee should bow, in heaven and on earth and under the earth, and every tongue confess that Jesus Christ is _________, to the glory of God the Father."

Philippians 2:9-11

37

Praise God for all that He is to you

Gracious Lord, to you I owe everything. I am alive because of the breath you sustain me with, and I am redeemed because of His life whom you saved me with. In every circumstance, I will give you thanks. With every gift, I will give you praise. For every ability, I will give you glory.

"Praise the Lord! Praise God in his sanctuary; praise him in his mighty heavens! Praise him for his mighty deeds; praise him according to his excellent greatness!" Psalm 150:1-2

"I appeal to you therefore, brothers, by the mercies of God, to present your bodies as a living sacrifice, holy and acceptable to God, which is your spiritual worship." Romans 12:1

Life Message

Once you have tasted the joy of knowing God, your craving for Him becomes inescapable. Knowing and experiencing the love of God produces within you *feelings of joy* that you long to speak back to Him through praise and worship. To praise God is to speak to Him in an expressive manner (through speech, song, dance, art, etc.) the joyful feelings His truths provoke. To worship God then is to allow your feelings of joy to generate joyful actions (righteous living and good works). Christian, it is important to note that feeling the presence of God is just as important as knowing the truth about God. Only through feeling the joy of knowing God is praise and worship made possible. Avail yourself to this feeling and express it to God through endless praise and worship.

"Praise the Lord! Praise God in his sanctuary; praise him in his mighty heavens! Praise him for his mighty deeds; praise him according to his excellent greatness!" Psalm 150:1-2

"I appeal to you therefore, brothers, by the mercies of God, to present your bodies as a living sacrifice, holy and acceptable to God, which is your spiritual worship." Romans 12:1

Day 37 I Prayer Session continues on following page

Jesus, you are worthy of my utmost praise and worship. Let me *feel* the joy of knowing and experiencing you so that your glorious presence becomes the source of my adoration and praise. **Hear my heart as I appreciate you for who you are and all you do...**

____

____

____

____

____

____

____

____

____

____

____

____

"_____________ the Lord! Praise God in his sanctuary; praise him in his mighty heavens! Praise him for his _____________ _____________; praise him according to his excellent greatness!" Psalm 150:1-2

"I appeal to you therefore, brothers, by the mercies of God, to present your _____________ as a _____________ _____________, holy and acceptable to God, which is your _____________ _____________."

Romans 12:1

38

Never Stop Confessing – Never Stop Repenting

Lord of Mercy, you became the offering for sin though you knew no sin. Your death on the cross was undeserving, yet you chose to die so I would not perish. Search me for sin and discipline me in what you find. Cleanse me of my unrighteousness so that I might fulfill your good purpose with my life.

"If we confess our sins, he is faithful and just to forgive us our sins and to cleanse us from all unrighteousness."
1 John 1:9

"Repent, therefore, and turn back, that your sins may be blotted out, that times of refreshing may come from the presence of the Lord." Acts 3:19

Life Message

Keep the faith you were called into. The assurance of your eternal salvation is solely evidenced by the Holy Spirit's active presence in your life. If you want to feel the joy of having eternal security, examine your life. *What do you desire? Are you feeding the desires of your flesh, or are you fighting against such desires and striving to live righteously?* Be aware, there is nothing mechanically automatic about eternal security wherein you say a prayer and heaven's door opens to you. Rather, there is a sense of perseverance required of you that guarantees your salvation. Just as God called you to new life, He also calls you to remain in that new life.

Never stop confessing

Sin is rebellion against God. No matter if it is the sin of a believer or an unbeliever, sin is rebellion. As a believer in Christ, when you rebel against God, your fellowship with Him becomes broken. Your sins distance you from God and keep you from experiencing the joy of His presence. Only by confessing your sins daily do you move toward God and allow Him to restore the fellowship you both share. Consider it like bathing; you bathe daily to remove that which makes you unclean. Spiritually speaking, you need to bathe daily in the blood of Christ (confess your sins and seek forgiveness) to remove the unrighteousness caused by your sin.

Never stop repenting

Following your admission of sin, repentance becomes a necessity. God calls you to repentance every day; His Word commands it. It is important for you to understand however, that repentance does not mean automatic perfection. Repentance often requires time and repetition to produce within you strength worthy of overcoming sin. The more often you repent of your sin, the looser sin's grip becomes. Therefore, in your fight to overcome sin, you must make repentance a practice and devote yourself to it.

"If we confess our sins, he is faithful and just to forgive us our sins and to cleanse us from all unrighteousness."
1 John 1:9

"Repent, therefore, and turn back, that your sins may be blotted out, that times of refreshing may come from the presence of the Lord." Acts 3:19

Jesus, I do not want to go on sinning. Remind me of the power I possess through your Holy Spirit and see to it that I align my desires with His so that I stop sinning. **Search me for every sin as I search myself. Forgive me; cleanse me of my unrighteousness; and revive the fellowship we share as I admit my sins and express to you my desire to repent...**

306

"If we _______________ our sins, he is faithful and just to _______________ us our sins and to cleanse us from all unrighteousness." 1 John 1:9

"_______________, therefore, and turn back, that your sins may be blotted out, that times of _______________ may come from the presence of the Lord." Acts 3:19

39

Glorify God by living in accordance with the Holy Spirit

My Father, anoint and fill me with the power of your Holy Spirit. Make way for Him to take root in my heart and produce within me seeds that bear much fruit.

"But the Helper, the Holy Spirit, whom the Father will send in my name, he will teach you all things and bring to your remembrance all that I have said to you."

John 14:26

"But you will receive power when the Holy Spirit has come upon you, and you will be my witnesses in Jerusalem and in all Judea and Samaria, and to the end of the earth."

Acts 1:8

Day 39 I Prayer Session continues on following page

Life Message

Being filled with the divine nature of the Holy Spirit is essential. Holy Spirit possesses every character trait and ability of God and manifests God's qualities and abilities to you as you call on Him to do so. In all your asking of God, consider your requests for **God's power** to be your ultimate pursuit; because being filled with the power of God will enable you to do the things God does.

Did you catch that?

The sovereign ruler of the universe who brought everything to life with the sound of His voice is willing to manifest His divine power to you through His Holy Spirit *if* you are willing to receive it!

What might you do with the power of God?

Invite God's power into your life daily by asking Him to anoint and fill you with His Holy Spirit. Determine to absorb God's divine nature into your heart and mind until God Himself transforms your character and empowers you to influence and impact the world in ways only made possible by Him.

"But the Helper, the Holy Spirit, whom the Father will send in my name, he will teach you all things and bring to your remembrance all that I have said to you." John 14:26

"But you will receive power when the Holy Spirit has come upon you,

and you will be my witnesses in Jerusalem and in all Judea

and Samaria, and to the end of the earth."

Acts 1:8

God, anoint and fill me with your Holy Spirit until your divine nature overflows from me. Liken my heart and mind to the heart and mind of Christ until everything I am is everything you are.

Hear my heart as I ask of you…

"But the Helper, the _________ ____________, whom the Father will
send in my name, he will teach you all things and bring to your
remembrance all that I have said to you."

John 14:26

"But you will receive ___________ when the Holy Spirit has come
upon you, and you will be ____ _______________ in Jerusalem and in
all Judea and Samaria, and to the end of the earth."

Acts 1:8

312

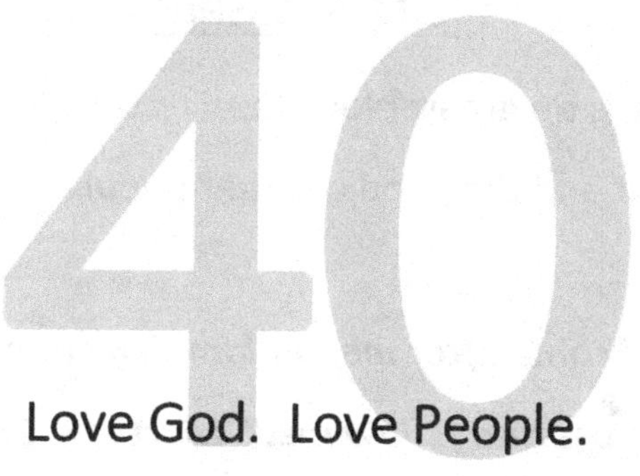

Love God. Love People.

Father, turn your ear to my intercessions for my fellow man. Grant eternal salvation to all who have yet to receive you, and bestow power and spiritual wisdom upon those who have. Fulfill your provisional promises in each of their lives, and see to it that they present themselves to you having been conformed to your deity on the Day of Judgment.

"Greater love has no one than this, that someone lay down his life for his friends."
John 15:13

"Go therefore and make disciples of all nations."
Matthew 28:19a

Day 40 I Prayer Session continues on following page

Life Message

Christian, there is no greater love than to lay your life down for the cause of Christ and the good of other people. Jesus says to you:

"If anyone would come after me, let him deny himself and take up his cross and follow me." Matthew 16:24

Do you have the courage and bravery to deny yourself for the cause of Christ and the benefit of others? Are you willing to sacrifice your plans, your comfort and your desires in order to live your life completely devoted to knowing, experiencing and sharing the love of God?

This is the path Jesus chose, and it is the path taken by every Christian who desires to make an eternal difference in the world. Recognize that you have one lifetime and one opportunity to do God's will on earth, and **there is no second chance.** Don't reflect on your life one day and wish you had developed a deeper faith, a deeper trust and a stronger love for God and His people—*do it now!* Fight to love God and love people. Pursue God through endless prayer and a steady absorption of His Word. Develop for yourself a personal ministry— one in which you commit to praying for people, enacting the works of God and sharing the love of Christ with others.

Believer, this is your moment in time. This is your one opportunity to impact the world for the cause of Christ.
Will you respond to His call?

"Greater love has no one than this, that someone lay down his life for his friends."

John 15:13

"Go therefore and make disciples of all nations."

Matthew 28:19a

Jesus, you have called me to be your image. You have entrusted me with faith and you have ordained me to proclaim your message and share your love with the world. Inspire me to deny myself, pick up my cross and follow you. Empower me to influence and impact the world and the people in it through prayer and through love demonstrated by taking action.

Hear my heart as I advocate for others; hear my heart as I determine to glorify you by pursuing your will...

____

____

____

____

____

____

____

____

____

____

____

____ Amen.

"________________ ________ has no one than this, that someone

lay down his life for his friends."

John 15:13

"Go therefore and _________ _____________________ of all nations."

Matthew 28:19a

Thank you for experiencing TALK TO JESUS

If you were blessed in some way, please consider positively rating and reviewing TALK TO JESUS on amazon.com, goodreads.com and other book review sites.

Review TALK TO JESUS on Amazon!

Six A's in Review

Approach > Acknowledge > Appreciate

Approach	Acknowledge	Appreciate
Humbly	*Who He Is*	*What He Has Done*
Gratefully	*Where He Is*	*What He Is Doing*
Righteously	*What He Does*	*What He Has Yet To Do*
Confidently		

Admit > Ask > Advocate

Admit	Ask	Advocate
Your Sins	*Eternal Regenerative Petitions*	*Believers*
& Repent	*Love • Joy • Peace*	*Non-believers*
	Patience • Kindness	*Family/Friends*
	Goodness • Faithfulness	*Classmates*
	Gentleness • Self Control	*Coworkers*
	Every attribute of Christ	*Leaders*
		Church Leaders
	Kingdom Minded Temporal Petitions	*Your Church*
	• Give us this day our daily bread	*Your Community*
	• Forgive our trespasses	*Your City*
	• Guard us from evil	*Your Nation*
		All Nations

TALK TO JESUS Reassessment

Circle the numbered response that you identify with most.

1. **Has prayer caused things to happen in your life that would not have happened if you had not prayed?**
   - 5 Absolutely
   - 4 I think so
   - 3 I am uncertain
   - 2 I do not think so
   - 1 No/I do not pray

2. **How much value and influence do you place on your prayers relative to God's unfolding plan for your life, for the lives of others and for the world in general?**
   - 5 I consider nothing more valuable or more influential than my prayers
   - 4 My prayers have some value and influence but not as much as I would like
   - 3 I am uncertain
   - 2 I do not think my prayers have much value or influence
   - 1 Prayer is useless

3. **Have you experienced a change in your character because of your praying?**
   - 5 Yes, I have experienced complete transformation through prayer
   - 4 I have experienced some character change through prayer, but not as much as I would like
   - 3 I am uncertain
   - 2 If I have experienced any character change, prayer has had little to do with it
   - 1 I have not experienced any change in my character by way of prayer

4. **Do you believe God wants you to pray?**

   5 God desires for me to be in an attitude of prayer every moment of every day

   4 God wants me to pray, but not necessarily all the time

   3 I am uncertain

   2 God does not care if I pray or if I do not pray

   1 God does not want me to pray

5. **Does God consider prayer a command worthy to obey?**

   5 Yes, God commands that I pray

   4 Prayer is a treasured gift from God but not a command from God

   3 I am uncertain

   2 God does not care if I pray or if I do not pray

   1 Prayer never reaches God

6. **By what means do you relate with God most?**

   5 Through prayer and meditation on God's Word

   4 Through prayer and my life experiences

   3 I am uncertain

   2 I do not relate with God often

   1 I do not have a relationship with God

7. **Do you designate a specific place and time to have uninterrupted/undistracted quality time spent alone with God?**

   5 Yes, I spend at least 30 minutes per day there

   4 No, but I occasionally pray when I wake up and/or before I go to sleep

   3 I am uncertain

   2 I pray sporadically throughout my day and/or while I am in my car

   1 I seldom pray/I do not pray

8. **How would you describe your prayer life?**

   5 My prayer life is exciting and spontaneous/
      I consider prayer to be my greatest adventure

   4 Prayer is something I look forward to each day

   3 I am uncertain

   2 My prayer life is not that exciting

   1 I do not pray

9. **Which statement do you identify with most?**

   5 I am dependent upon God and His provisions the way a
      toddler is dependent upon his or her caretaker

   4 I rely on God and use the talents, skills and abilities He
      provides to procure my good future

   3 I am uncertain

   2 I have worked hard for what I have achieved, and I thank
      God for it

   1 I alone am responsible for my success

10. **Which statement do you identify with most?**

   5 I experience complete satisfaction daily

   4 Sometimes I wish life offered me a bit more

   3 I am uncertain

   2 I deserve to receive just as much as I give

   1 I am not happy with my life

11. **Which statement do you identify with most?**

   5 Every decision I make is obedient to God and His Word

   4 I try my best to discern God's will prior to making a decision

   3 I am uncertain

   2 God is on my side therefore I know He will redirect my path
      if I make a poor decision

   1 I do what I want to do when I want to do it

12. **Which statement do you identify with most?**

   5   I have experienced firsthand the miraculous power of God

   4   I believe God has power to perform miracles and I have seen and/or heard of such miracles

   3   I am uncertain

   2   God may be able to perform miracles but He does so a lot less often than I would if I were God

   1   God does not perform miracles

13. **How often do you obey God's commands?**

   5   Every waking moment

   4   Most of the time

   3   I am uncertain

   2   I deeply struggle with sin

   1   I choose not to obey God

14. **Which statement do you identify with most?**

   5   I cheerfully and regularly invest a healthy portion of the money I earn into building God's kingdom and advancing the Gospel

   4   I sometimes invest a portion of the money I earn into building God's kingdom and advancing the Gospel

   3   I am uncertain

   2   I am content with who I give my money to and how much I give

   1   I do not trust the church enough to give them my money

15. **Which statement do you identify with most?**

   5   My sin keeps me from experiencing the joy of fellowshipping with God

   4   My sin puts a strain on my conscience

   3   I am uncertain

   2   My sin does not cause me to feel any negative emotions

   1   I do not sin

16. **What is your general attitude relative to what you receive in life (be it material possessions or otherwise)?**

    5 Prayer is the primary factor for me receiving or not receiving blessings from God

    4 Because God is good, I receive

    3 I am uncertain

    2 God will provide everything I need whether I ask Him or not

    1 I alone am responsible for everything I receive or do not receive

17. **Which statement do you identify with most?**

    5 People experience change daily as a result of my praying and they thank me for it

    4 People have told me that their life has been affected by my prayers

    3 I am uncertain

    2 I enjoy praying for other people

    1 I do not pray for other people

18. **How many passages of scripture have you retained (committed to present memory)?**

    5 I have retained more than 1,000 passages of scripture

    4 I have retained more than 500 passages of scripture

    3 I am uncertain

    2 I have retained more than 100 passages of scripture

    1 I have retained a handful of scriptures/ I have not committed any scriptures to memory

19. **Which statement do you identify with most?**

> **5** I meditate daily on many of the more than 1,000 passages of scriptures I have committed to memory
>
> **4** I meditate daily on many of the more than 500 passages of scripture I have committed to memory
>
> **3** When I read the Bible, I pause to absorb certain passages of scripture into my mind before progressing further in my reading
>
> **2** I read the Bible
>
> **1** I do not read the Bible

20. **Combine your scores for questions 18 & 19 and divide the combined score by two: _______ ← this is your score for question 20.** (For example, if you scored a 2 on question 18, and a 3 on question 19, your score for question 20 is 2.5). *Question 20 pertains to responding to God's Word. Responding to God's Word is more likely to occur if God's Word is committed to memory and meditated on regularly.*

***Before totaling your final score, consider giving response to the questions you marked 'I am uncertain'.**

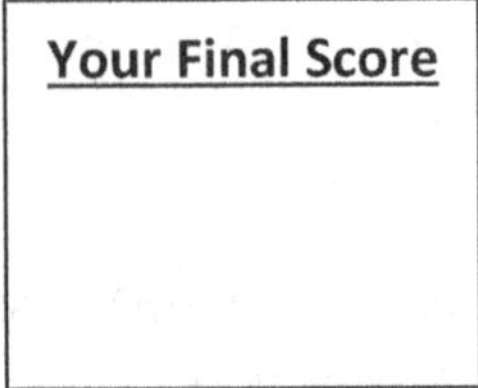

Consider experiencing TALK TO JESUS 1-2 times per year

as you develop a life and ministry of fervent, unceasing prayer.

100 - 80 | Consider God's Word written for you in **Philippians 3:12-21**

79 - 60 | Consider God's Word written for you in **Psalm 27:4**

59-20 | Consider God's Word written for you in **John 3:16-21**

LEADER/MENTOR RESOURCES

Discussion Questions | Note Taking

40 Day Journey

Group Leader | Group Mentor
Begin and end each meeting with prayer

Week One | Meeting One
Book Introduction

*Consider reading aloud (as a group) the opening pages of
TALK TO JESUS beginning with **Individuals | Partners | Small Groups**
through **TALK TO JESUS Assessment Overview**.
Complete the **TALK TO JESUS Assessment**.*

Discussion Questions

> **What is prayer to you?**

(How do you define prayer | What does prayer mean for you)

> **Have you received Jesus for who He truly is?**

(Describe the circumstances and experiences that led you to

Christ)

> **On which questions did you score – 5?**

> **On which questions did you score – 1, 2, 3 or 4?**

(Why did you choose this numbered response | Consider

highlighting/circling the Subjects/Days of Focus to which you

plan to give special attention | see page 14)

> **Group Members – Following today's meeting, begin**

> **experiencing your 40 Day Journey by reading and**

> **experiencing Day 1**

Notes

Discussion Questions

- **Consider sharing your remembrance of a time (or the first time) you called out to God and He answered your prayer?** (What was your situation and circumstance | How did God respond | Day 1)

- **Which attribute of the Holy Spirit have you chosen to be filled with and enriched by?** (Why did you choose this attribute | What do you hope is accomplished by God and you through your praying for this attribute | Day 3)

- **For whom have you chosen to pray?** (Why are you choosing to pray for this person | What do you hope is accomplished by God and you through your praying for this person | Day 3)

- **At what place and time(s) are you spending quality time with God in uninterrupted prayer?** (Why did you choose this place and time | How is it going | Is God responding to your prayer | Day 4)

Notes

Week Three | Meeting Three
Days 8-14

<u>Discussion Questions</u>

- ➤ **Consider sharing your personal prayer motivated by Jesus' Model Prayer spoken in Matthew 6:9-13.** (Day 9)

- ➤ **Do you have any questions or comments related to the Talk To Jesus Prayer Session Matrix?** (Day 10)

- ➤ **What talent, gift and ability did you list on Day 11? | How might your life be different had God not provided for you the talents, gifts and abilities you embody?** (Day 11 | Day 12)

- ➤ **In what areas of your life can you more richly offer God the gratitude He deserves?** (Day 12)

- ➤ **Consider sharing your negative thoughts and their truth replacements.** (Day 13)

Feel free to share in the group setting or with a partner.

Notes

Week Four | Meeting Four
Days 15-21

<u>Discussion Questions</u>

➢ **GROUP PRAYER – Consider spending time in group prayer acknowledging God for who He is, where He is and all He does.**

(Beginning with the letter A and ending at Z, acknowledge God together | One by one, each group member take a moment to pray aloud acknowledging God by *naming and exalting Him* using a specific letter of the alphabet)

➢ **How have you grown spiritually through the first half of your 40 Day Journey?**

(In what ways is God speaking to you and in what ways are you responding to Him | What changes have you experienced thus far as a result of the knowledge, wisdom and insights you are receiving through your 40 Day Journey with Christ)

➢ **Group Leader/Group Mentor: Share with group members your experience in leading/mentoring people through TALK TO JESUS.**

(Encourage group members to consider becoming a Group Leader/Mentor for people who have yet to experience TALK TO JESUS | Encourage group members to write down the names of 5-10 people whom they would like to lead/mentor through Pathway To God and/or the 40 Day Journey)

Week Four | Meeting Four

Notes

Discussion Questions

> **What gift from God have you chosen to begin managing more responsibly?**
>
> (Why did you choose this gift | How have you begun to change the way you manage this gift from God | Day 22)

> **GROUP PRAYER – Consider confessing your sins to one another and to God.** *Leader/Mentor take the lead.*
>
> *Read aloud James 5:16: "Therefore confess your sins to one another, that you may be healed. The prayer of a righteous person has great power as it is working."*
>
> *Read aloud 2 Chronicles 7:14: "If my people who are called by my name humble themselves, and pray and seek my face and turn from their wicked ways, then I will hear from heaven and will forgive their sin and heal their land."*
>
> (Confess your sins to one another | Seek forgiveness together)

> **GROUP PRAYER – Seek God for His power, His attributes and His righteousness.**
>
> (As a group, ask God for a renewed filling of His own attributes | Seek the power of God, the gifts of the Spirit and the ability to boldly share the Gospel of Christ with others | Encourage each group member to join in praying)

336

Notes

Week Six | Meeting Six
Days 29-34

<u>Discussion Questions</u>

> **In what ways are you becoming the answer to your prayers for the person for whom you have been praying?**
>
> (Have you told this person you have been praying on his/her behalf | If so, what was his/her response | Day 29)

> **What does it look like to reveal God's glory in the way you think, feel, speak, behave and act?**
>
> (In what ways are you revealing God's glory to the people around you | In what ways are you not | Day 31)

> **Have you memorized and meditated on 1 John 3:18?**
>
> (Recite 1 John 3:18 aloud | Describe what this passage of scripture means for you personally | Day 32 | Day 33)

> **How are you responding to God's Word written in 1 John 3:18?** (How might you enact the love of God—back to God, to yourself and other people | Day 34)

338

Notes

Week Seven | Meeting Seven
Days 35-40

<u>Discussion Questions</u>

- How has your prayer life changed as a result of your 40 Day Journey?

- In what ways are you experiencing a closer relationship with God following your TALK TO JESUS journey?

- How do you envision your walk with God as you move forward?

- Have you joined the Talk To Jesus movement?

  Become a TALK TO JESUS Member and let us as an organization equip you with a ministry platform designed to empower you as you enact the works of Christ in and around your community.

  (Visit t2j.org and join the TALK TO JESUS movement)

- Do you desire to become a Talk To Jesus Leader/Mentor?

  Host a TALK TO JESUS group!

  (Become a Group Leader/Mentor and lead others through Pathway To God and/or the 40 Day Journey)

Notes

Leader/Mentor Final Thoughts

Pathway To God

Group Leader | Group Mentor
Begin and end each meeting with prayer

Week One | Meeting One
Book Introduction

*Consider reading aloud (as a group) the opening pages of TALK TO JESUS beginning with **Individuals | Partners | Small Groups** through **TALK TO JESUS Assessment Overview**.*
*Complete the **TALK TO JESUS Assessment**.*

Discussion Questions

➢ **Why are you choosing to experience Pathway To God?**

(Do you sense God calling out to you through your life experiences, through another person and/or through His Word)

➢ **What thoughts and feelings arise as you read John 14:6 and John 6:35?** (Test Yourself | Page 6)

➢ **On which questions did you score – 5?**

➢ **On which questions did you score – 1, 2, 3 or 4?**

(Why did you choose this numbered response | How do you feel about your final score)

➢ **Group Members – Following today's meeting, begin experiencing Day 1 of Pathway To God by speaking to and hearing from your Creator**

Week One | Meeting One

Notes

Let the Word of God speak

Believing the following passages of scripture to be the Word of God (that is, recognizing and understanding these messages as 'God speaking to you'), what thoughts and feelings arise as you hear from Him?

- ➤ **"So God created man in His own image, in the image of God he created him; male and female he created them." Genesis 1:27** (What thoughts and feelings arise as you reflect on God telling you that you are His creation | Day 1)

- ➤ **"For by him all things were created, in heaven and on earth, visible and invisible, whether thrones or dominions or rulers or authorities – all things were created through him and for him." Colossians 1:16** (What thoughts and feelings arise as you reflect on God telling you that you are created *for* Him | Day 2)

- ➤ **"…for all have sinned and fall short of the glory of God." Romans 3:23** (What are you doing or not doing that causes you to fall short of God's glory | Day 3)

- ➤ **"God shows his love for us in that while we were still sinners, Christ died for us." Romans 5:8 | "For God so loved the world, that he gave his one and only Son, that whoever believes in him should not perish but have eternal life." John 3:16** (What do these scriptures reveal to you about the love of God | Day 7)

Notes

Let the Word of God speak

Believing the following passages of scripture to be the Word of God (that is, recognizing and understanding these messages as 'God speaking to you'), what thoughts and feelings arise as you hear from Him?

- **"And there is salvation in no one else [but Jesus], for there is no other name under heaven given among men by which we must be saved." Romans 3:25** (What thoughts and feelings arise as you hear God telling you that *Jesus* is the way to salvation | Day 9)

- **"Repent therefore, and turn back, that your sins may be blotted out, that times of refreshing may come from the presence of the Lord, and that he may send the Christ appointed for you." Acts 3:19-20** (What thoughts and feelings arise as you hear God telling you that you must turn away from what you know to be wrong in order to receive Jesus and experience eternal salvation | Day 9)

- **Have you confessed your sins, repented from what you know to be sinful, and chosen to receive Jesus as your Savior and Lord? Is God calling on you to do so?** *Leader/Mentor: Read aloud Day 10.* (If you have received Jesus in this manner, proclaim it to the group! | If you would like to receive Jesus, profess it to God in the company of your group! | If you have not/choose not to, be encouraged to continue calling out to God asking Him to reveal to you—*Jesus*)

Notes

Made in the USA
Monee, IL
15 July 2025